UNEXPECTED
NEWS

UNEXPECTED NEWS

*Reading the Bible
with Third World Eyes*

ROBERT McAFEE BROWN

THE WESTMINSTER PRESS
Philadelphia

Book design by Alice Derr

First edition

Published by The Westminster Press®
Philadelphia, Pennsylvania

PRINTED IN THE UNITED STATES OF AMERICA
9 8 7 6 5 4 3 2 1

Library of Congress Cataloging in Publication Data

Brown, Robert McAfee, 1920–
    Unexpected news.

    Bibliography: p.
    1. Bible—Criticism, interpretation, etc. 2. Christianity
—Developing countries. 3. Church and social problems.
I. Title.
BS511.2.B77 1984   220.6   84-2380
ISBN 0-664-24552-8 (pbk.)

ACKNOWLEDGMENTS

Grateful acknowledgment is made to the following for the use of copyrighted material:

National Council of the Churches of Christ in the U.S.A., for quotations from the Revised Standard Version of the Bible copyrighted 1946, 1952, © 1971, 1973 by the Division of Christian Education of the National Council of the Churches of Christ in the U.S.A.

The New York Times, for quotation from "The New Effort to Control Information" by Floyd Abrams, September 25, 1983. Copyright © 1983 by The New York Times Company. Reprinted by permission.

NICM Journal, for permission to reprint, in Chapter 1, portions of my essay "The Boundary Area Between Biblical Perspectives and Religious Studies," in the Summer 1981 issue (Vol. 6, No. 3).

Religion and Literature, for permission to reprint, in Chapter 3, portions of my essay "The Nathan Syndrome: Stories with a Moral Intention," in the Spring 1984 issue.

Sequoia: The Church at Work, newspaper of the Northern California Ecumenical Council, for permission to quote from an article by Krin Van Tatenhove in the September 1983 issue.

The Westminster Press, for the exchange at the end of Chapter 5, which was first published in my book *Theology in a New Key,* Copyright © 1978 The Westminster Press. Reprinted by permission.

Special thanks to
Philip Scharper
John Eagleson
Miguel d'Escoto, M.M.
without whose vision
Orbis Books would never have been created . . .

. . . and if Orbis Books had never been created
the rest of us might still be
reading the Bible
from a first world perspective
unaware that the Bible
cannot be contained within any perspective
but is
always bursting the bonds
within which we try to imprison it

CONTENTS

INTRODUCTION:
WHAT THIS BOOK IS ABOUT

A retired Air Force major, now a seminarian, went to a conference on "The Church and Central Africa." As the talks proceeded, he got angry. One speaker, he reports, "was basically saying that the United States is greatly responsible for the suffering in third world countries. Many of us were asking, 'What does this have to do with the Christian outlook?' "

The major was not suggesting that suffering in third world countries is alien to "the Christian outlook." What angered him was the suggestion that those of us who live in the United States are responsible for the suffering.

To his credit, the major didn't pack up and go home but went back to hear the African speaker a second time. His outlook was modified:

> [The speaker] was showing us that our imperialism is often unconscious, done through economic arrangement. As Christians who have compassion we need to know these facts, even if they hurt. I came away from the conference hurting in some ways, realizing that some of the things I have stood for aren't that good. For instance, when we talk of a "free market" we should at least realize that we are in it for ourselves, and often, Third World countries can't compete.
>
> I came away . . . with a deeper awareness that we have

to attempt to see the world the way others do. They won't
change just because we want them to.

(Cited in *Sequoia,* Northern California Ecumenical
Council, September 1983, pp. 5, 7)

The pages that follow are an attempt to take the major's
concern seriously and "see the world the way others do." Our
initial resource will be a group of people who look at the world
in ways very different from our own, the biblical writers. As
Christians who take the Bible seriously, we have an obligation
to compare our view of the world with theirs. The title and
subtitle of this book reflect that obligation.

The title *Unexpected News* suggests that when we turn to the
Bible, the "news" we find is always "unexpected": religious
people are often put down (scribes, Pharisees, and church folk);
worship is attacked (Amos); pagans are described as doing
God's will (Isaiah); great spiritual leaders get angry with God
(Job, Jeremiah); God's clearest message is communicated
through the obscure life of a criminal (Jesus of Nazareth). It is
certainly not the way we would have written the script.

What we are encountering is what Swiss theologian Karl
Barth described many years ago in an essay entitled "The
Strange New World Within the Bible." Barth discovered that
when he approached the Bible, every bit of spiritual and mental
equipment he brought to the task was shattered by that "strange
new world" and that as a result he had to begin looking at both
the Bible and his own world in a new way.

Barth's experience in 1917 is also our experience in 1984, and
the phenomenon is nothing new. Confrontation with the Bible
was shattering in A.D. 386, as Augustine discovered; in 1517, as
Martin Luther discovered; in 1934, as the German Confessing
Church discovered; in 1968, as Catholic bishops at Medellín,
Colombia, discovered. The world of the Bible is always a
"strange new world," and for that reason it is always communicating "unexpected news."

Christians make the initially bizarre gamble that "the strange new world within the Bible" is a more accurate view of the world than our own and that we have to modify our views as a result. This means engaging in dialogue with the Bible— bringing our questions to it, hearing its questions to us, examining our answers in its light, and taking its answers very seriously, particularly when they conflict with our own, which will be most of the time.

That is already a complicated exercise. But it is further complicated by the fact that we must be in dialogue not only with the Bible but also with Christians in other parts of the world who read the Bible in a very different way. In the following pages I will refer to them as "third world Christians." The term "third world" gained currency at an international conference at Bandung in 1955, where unaligned nations, who did not want to be considered satellites of either the United States (the "first world") or the Soviet Union (the "second world"), chose to describe themselves by contrast as the "third world." The term "third world Christians" will be a shorthand device to stand for something like "Christians living in Asia, Africa, Latin America, or impoverished areas of the United States, who are generally poor and powerless, victims of political and social and economic structures (usually supported by the U.S. government) that oppress them on all levels of their lives, while those same structures support and enrich us." The need for economy of wording is self-evident.

The term, however, is far from satisfactory, and even while using it I must apologize for it, since it not only sounds demeaning ("third world" = third rate?) but lumps in one category all kinds of diverse peoples. A more accurate designation would be "two-thirds world," since the number of those who suffer deprivation and oppression at the hands of the rest of us is at least two thirds, if not more, of the human family.

Significant Christian voices are being heard in the third world today. And when third world Christians listen to the Bible, *they hear different things than we hear.* It often seems as though they and we are reading different books. Why is this so?

Third world Christians think that people like us read the Bible from the vantage point of our privilege and comfort and screen out those parts that threaten us. They tell us that the basic viewpoint of the biblical writers is that of victims, those who have been cruelly used by society, the poor and oppressed. They further tell us that they are the contemporary counterparts of those biblical victims, cruelly used by contemporary society, the poor and oppressed. Consequently, when they hear the Bible offering hope and liberation to the oppressed of the ancient world, they hear hope and liberation being offered to them as the oppressed of the contemporary world. If God sided with the oppressed back then, they believe God continues to side with the oppressed here and now.

Is that what the Bible is really all about? Enough third world Christians are saying so, and living changed lives as a result, to impel us to explore the matter and see whether there might be a new word for us as well. We will do this by taking ten familiar biblical episodes and trying to see them through new eyes. The passages have been chosen both because they are important to third world Christians and because they are familiar to us. The texts give us a common meeting ground to compare different interpretations. As we see how others read the Bible, we may get a new understanding of what the biblical message says to us. For reasons of space, we will confine our dialogue partners chiefly to Latin America, but similar partners could be found in Asia and Africa as well.

The point of this book, then, is to encourage Bible study. It is not an end in itself but a means to another end: directly confronting the biblical text. It is not trying to be "balanced" but to be provocative, and readers are encouraged to challenge its particular interpretations; after all, the biblical texts are there, and it is the biblical texts that are important.

Each chapter begins with a statement of some aspect of our

situation that needs fresh attention in the light of biblical faith. This is followed by a biblical passage and some comments on ways of understanding the passage today. A third section provides other biblical materials elaborating the same theme. A final section raises questions and poses items for group discussion, since insights of others can often correct strange interpretations of our own. The "mix" and proportions within that overall framework vary from chapter to chapter. After all, a book about "unexpected news" should contain some surprises of its own.

Although I am not a professional biblical scholar, I dare to tread in contested areas because I believe that the message of the Bible is not limited to specialists but is open to all Christians, whether possessing the requisite degrees or not. As the specialists write more books raising the kinds of questions this one does, I will cheerfully relinquish the field and be content to learn from them.

The approach in these pages is close to what is sometimes called secondary naïveté. There is a primary naïveté that accepts everything in Scripture at face value and digs in its heels when portions of the Bible threaten to be eroded by the acids of modernity. Ax heads that float? No problem, the Bible says they floated.

From that position, a good many people, myself included, demur. By contrast, we have spent years examining the Bible with every possible variety of fine-tooth comb. We have dated manuscripts, challenged traditional authorships, rearranged the order of verses, corrected mistranslations of passages dear to childhood memory. After all that critical scrutiny, however, we have returned to the text itself, looking at it with a secondary naïveté, for we still have to ask the pesky question of the text as it stands, "What does the passage say to us?" If the passage contains material about an angel, the basic question at this point is not "Are there such things as angels, and do they conform to

the laws of aerodynamics?" but "Granting that the writer be-
lieved in angels as messengers of God, what message is God
trying to communicate through a story about an angel?"

Did Mary sing the Magnificat in the form in which it has
come down to us? Probably not. But such an answer does not
complete a discussion of Luke 1:46–55. We still have to ask,
"What does it mean for our faith that the Magnificat has been
preserved in this form and that its unsettling words have been
placed on the lips of Mary?" Unless we deal with such a question, we will find a dozen reasons to evade its revolutionary
message, falsely assuring ourselves that it was softly spoken by
a demure maiden with no fire in her eye.

So we are going to approach these stories as they now stand,
entering the world their tellers inhabited, to see if God can cut
through from their world to ours. What we hear will be "unexpected," and therefore upsetting, but at least it will never be
dull.

My final word is one of gratitude to all those sisters and
brothers in the third world—those noted in the text and those
who for their own survival must remain anonymous—whose
reading of the Bible has forced my own rereading of the Bible.
Part of me wishes I had never heard of them, for the rereading
has made the Bible a new book for me, much more disturbing
and continually challenging a lifetime of hard-won assumptions.
But as the process of reeducation and recommitment goes on,
I now see connections I never saw before between the God of
the Bible and the good news of "liberation for the oppressed."
To the degree that I stand in the way of that liberation I must
be challenged—by the oppressed and by God. But to the degree
that I can begin, in however timid ways, to be used by God in
a liberating process initially so threatening to folks like me, I too
am liberated. At least I am beginning to be able to name the sin
from which the Bible tells me I need liberation: complacency.

I am indebted to David Steele for some of the impetus in exploring the David and Nathan story.

In Scripture quotations, inclusive wording has been substituted for masculine pronouns.

R.M.B.

Heath, Massachusetts
Autumn 1983

If you are neutral in a situation of injustice, you have chosen the side of the oppressor. If an elephant has his foot on the tail of the mouse, and you say you are neutral, the mouse will not appreciate your neutrality.

—Desmond Tutu,
bishop of the Church
of the Province of South Africa (Anglican)

Me don' understand politics, me don' understand big words like "democratic socialism." What me say is what de Bible say, but because people don' read de Bible no more, dey tink me talk politics. Ha! It's de Bible what have it written and it strong, it powerful.

—Bob Marley, Jamaican folksinger

Reading the Bible with the eyes of the poor is a different thing from reading it with a full belly. If it is read in the light of the experience and hopes of the oppressed, the Bible's revolutionary themes—promise, exodus, resurrection and spirit—come alive.

—Jürgen Moltmann
The Church in the Power of the Spirit

1. EMMAUS . . . AND BACK AGAIN:
A NEW FORM OF KNOWING
(Changing Methods)

Luke 24:13–35

Our society puts a premium on knowing. Futurists tell us that we are moving from "the industrial society" to "the information society." The image for our age is no longer the foundry or the assembly line, but the microcomputer chip. Silicon, not steel, is where it's at.

But our immediate question is not "How do we process information now that computers have made it so easy?" but "How do we acquire knowledge in the first place? How do we learn? How do we gain the kind of wisdom by means of which to act appropriately? *How are knowing and doing related?*"

There is a long tradition in our culture that we should first build up a body of information, insights, and principles, in as detached a way as possible, and then apply them to the matter at hand. Keep cool, we are told, and don't act rashly.

Christians have done the same thing: first principles, then application; first wisdom, then deeds; first theology, then action. The principle, let us say, is "love"; how do we apply it in the Middle East? The principle is "justice"; what does that mean in the Bronx? The principle is "do good and avoid evil"; how do we relate that to Nicaragua? It's sometimes called the "banking method." Let others instruct us so that we can build up knowledge, in the same way that capital is accumulated in a bank account, and then draw on it as needed. Carrying on the image, we see that theology is even called the *depositum fidei,* the "deposit of faith," from which we can draw when necessary. But there is a catch: if we so choose, we can always postpone the jump from thought to action. We really need to acquire more information, read another book, attend one more conference, hold further conversations, in order to "clarify the issues." *Then* we'll act. So if the action looks risky, there is always a good reason to postpone it: we don't know enough yet.

We are fooling ourselves: we never actually "postpone" the jump from thought to action. For, paradoxical as it sounds, *not* to act *is* to act. It is to act by default for whoever is in charge. People who did not oppose the Nazi gassing of Jews were supporting the Nazis: "See," Hitler could say, "nobody is objecting." People who do not oppose United States support of military regimes in Central America are legitimating the murders committed by those regimes: "See," our administration can say, "nobody is objecting."

Christians in the third world are trying to relate thinking and doing in a different way. For them, as Gustavo Gutiérrez, a Roman Catholic priest in Peru, has said, "Theology is always the *second* act," not the first. What comes first is commitment, which in his situation means commitment to, and involvement with, the poor and oppressed. It is *in the midst* of the struggle of the poor for justice that theological reflection takes place. There is an ongoing relationship between "reflection and action" in which each continually informs and empowers the other: the more fully we act, the more fruitfully we can reflect on the meaning of our action and find ways to act more effectively next time; the more deeply we reflect, the more fruitfully we can embody the reflection in action and learn to reflect still more effectively. It is a process that never ends.

Which comes first? That is a kind of chicken-and-egg conundrum. We never act *or* reflect in a vacuum: thought always precedes action, action always precedes thought. So the question is not "Which comes first?" but *"Which is basic?"* And third world Christians have a clear answer to that question: it is action, engagement, involvement that is basic. Theology that does not grow out of commitment is suspect.

This is something of a shock to those of us who have been taught to put a high premium on "bias-free" intellectualizing, with our emotions and commitments kept strictly under control. Surely it gives all that away to stack the cards in favor of this "new" approach.

But the approach is not so new after all. Neglected, perhaps, but not new. It bears a remarkable resemblance to a biblical approach to knowing, and we shall explore it in what might seem an unlikely place for "a theory of knowledge"—the account of a resurrection appearance. And yet perhaps the place is not so unlikely after all, for if anything could ever challenge our conventional ways of knowing, it would surely be the unprecedented report of a raising from the dead.

THE BIBLICAL TEXT: LUKE 24:13–35

[13]That very day two of them were going to a village named Emmaus, about seven miles from Jerusalem, [14]and talking with each other about all these things that had happened. [15]While they were talking and discussing together, Jesus himself drew near and went with them. [16]But their eyes were kept from recognizing him. [17]And he said to them, "What is this conversation which you are holding with each other as you walk?" And they stood still, looking sad. [18]Then one of them, named Cleopas, answered him, "Are you the only visitor to Jerusalem who does not know the things that have happened there in these days?" [19]And he said to them, "What things?" And they said to him, "Concerning Jesus of Nazareth, who was a prophet mighty in deed and word before God and all the people, [20]and how our chief priests and rulers delivered him up to be condemned to death and crucified him. [21]But we had hoped that he was the one to redeem Israel. Yes, and besides all this, it is now the third day since this happened.

¹²Moreover, some women of our company amazed us. They were at the tomb early in the morning ²³and did not find his body; and they came back saying that they had even seen a vision of angels, who said that he was alive. ²⁴Some of those who were with us went to the tomb, and found it just as the women had said; but him they did not see." ²⁵And he said to them, "O foolish men, and slow of heart to believe all that the prophets have spoken! ²⁶Was it not necessary that the Christ should suffer these things and enter into his glory?" ²⁷And beginning with Moses and all the prophets, he interpreted to them in all the scriptures the things concerning himself.

²⁸So they drew near to the village to which they were going. He appeared to be going further, ²⁹but they constrained him, saying, "Stay with us, for it is toward evening and the day is now far spent." So he went in to stay with them. ³⁰When he was at table with them, he took the bread and blessed, and broke it, and gave it to them. ³¹And their eyes were opened and they recognized him; and he vanished out of their sight. ³²They said to each other, "Did not our hearts burn within us while he talked to us on the road, while he opened to us the scriptures?" ³³And they rose that same hour and returned to Jerusalem; and they found the eleven gathered together and those who were with them, ³⁴who said, "The Lord has risen indeed, and has appeared to Simon!" ³⁵Then they told what had happened on the road, and how he was known to them in the breaking of the bread.

There has been a lot of heavy stuff going on, and two of Jesus' disciples, deeply committed to him and to the poor with whom he has aligned himself, are walking to Emmaus and reflecting on the action-packed week just concluded. They are confused and fearful. Their leader has been murdered, and they have not acquitted themselves too nobly in the surrounding tumult.

Just a week ago there had been the first-century equivalent of a ticker-tape parade welcoming a hero home, but from that promising beginning it had been downhill all the way. There had been a number of disastrous confrontations with the authorities, who had seemed determined to get Jesus by whatever means they could. There had been the chilling suspicion, and finally the clear knowledge, that there was an informer in their midst, even an *agent provocateur.* There had been the appearance of the Tac Squad in Gethsemane and the disciples' cop-out as they all ran away from the scene. After the arrest there had been a phony trial, with bribed witnesses and a lot of confusion about which court had jurisdiction in the case, followed by an unphony scourging, as the cops roughed Jesus up and worked him over in jail. Finally there had been the act of capital punishment, Jesus' execution on the city dump heap in the first-century equivalent of an electric chair. Pretext: his death was necessary for the maintenance of law and order, to keep the crime rate down. The placard over the place of execution had identified him as a subversive.

And as if that were not enough to cope with, confusing rumors were going around town that the executed leader had risen from the dead. Some women had gone to the tomb that very morning and reported that the body was missing. But Luke, with breathtaking honesty, in a passage just before the beginning of our text, reports that the male disciples did not take the women's report seriously: "These words," he tells us, "seemed to them an idle tale, and they did not believe them" (Luke 24:11) —which only proves that within a few hours of its creation the Christian church was guilty of male chauvinism.

In events growing out of that background, we can distinguish —in addition to the subsequent vindication of the women—four steps that provide a new approach to knowing and doing.

1. The disciples' first question, not unnaturally, is *"What is going on here?"* They do not say "Let's construct an epistemology" or "Let's establish an overall framework within which to reason together." No, as Luke puts it, they are "talking with each other about all these things that had happened" (Luke

24:14). They are reflecting abut their previous actions, actions that have turned out disastrously. Not only that, but they are scared stiff. They have been living behind locked doors. After all, if the Committee on Un-Roman Activities has disposed of their leader, won't the followers be next? Jesus had said something a few weeks earlier about crosses for everybody (see Chapter 8), and Rome's first rule in dealing with subversive organizations is to wipe them out as completely as possible, so that no little remnants can regroup and reorganize.

The disciples' attempt to answer the question "What is going on here?" is not successful. They have misread the evidence. "We had hoped," they reflect, "that he would be the one to redeem Israel." But Israel has not been redeemed. Indeed, their leader has confronted Israel's enemies and been wiped out in a five-day blitz. On an earlier occasion, Jesus had chastised those who could make accurate weather predictions but did not know how to "discern the signs of the times" (Matt. 16:3)—an apt description of their present plight. Something is missing.

2. Part of what is missing is supplied by the second stage of the story. A stranger appears and walks along with them while they air their perplexity. He seems to be some sort of rabbi or teacher. Suddenly we have a seminar situation: two students and a teacher, a student-faculty ratio lavish enough to make modern educators green with envy, though it would strike terror to the heart of any budget-conscious administrator.

The teacher is stern. "Foolish men," he berates them, "and slow of heart to believe all that the prophets have spoken!" (Luke 24:25). And then he begins with Moses and the prophets and interprets the things in the Jewish Scriptures that will clarify what has been going on. He says to them in effect, *"If you want to know what is going on now, you have to know what went on before.* If you want to understand the present, you must understand the past. If you want to know what it means to be a Jew today, you'll have to reflect on what it meant to be a Jew in Moses' time, in Isaiah's time, in Jeremiah's time."

That's some help, and it must have raised the level of the discussion. If Jesus was the one to "redeem Israel" and they are confused about that, now they can pursue the matter more fully and with more background material. To "redeem" would mean to draw people together, to set them on a new path, to reconcile and heal, to usher in a new era of compassion and understanding and justice. They know the words now, and they have a clearer intellectual understanding of what is at stake.

3. But it still is not enough. The reflection must turn to action, and it does so in the third stage of the story. As they approach their destination, the village of Emmaus, it is clear to the disciples that the stranger (whose identity is still hidden from them) intends to go further. So what do they do? They invite him to dinner.

It is the turning point. For instead of continuing to *talk* about redemption, they *act it out;* they engage in a redeeming deed, inviting a total stranger to share a meal. Their action changes the stranger from a stranger to a companion—in the most literal sense of the word, for "companion" (from the Latin words *cum* and *panis*) means "with bread." A companion is one with whom to share bread. The shift is from truth talked about to truth lived out, from reflection to action.

And only now do things begin to fall into place. Only at this point do the two disciples learn the identity of the stranger, and that takes a corresponding action on his part. Only when they break bread together, when they move from words to deeds, does clarity come. He was not known to them in the discussions on the road, Luke reports, "he was known to them in the breaking of the bread" (Luke 24:35). What they now receive through Jesus' action is not more information but a new relationship. Notice further that the new awareness the disciples have is awareness not only about the present moment but about the past as well. They see not only what is happening around

the table but what was happening along the road, even though
at the time they had been too dense to take it in. "Did not our
hearts burn within us?" they reflect later on. This happened not
only when he broke the bread but "while he talked to us on the
road, while he opened to us the scriptures" (Luke 24:32). Now
they know for the first time what was really going on back then.
The present enacting of the truth gives life and power to the
previous discussion of the truth. The action deepens the reflection.

4. But we are not quite at the end. There is a fourth stage in
the story: Jesus vanishes.

Probably any twentieth-century person has difficulty with the
biology of that claim; bodies simply don't "vanish" that way.
Yet we should not have too much difficulty with the *theology* of
the claim, which is a way of telling us that once the moment of
insight has been achieved around the table, the action is no
longer around the table. The action is somewhere else.

The disciples are not given the privilege of sitting around for
the rest of the evening, lifting their glasses and saying, "Wow!
Have we ever had a fantastic religious experience!" (or, as they
might have put it if they had been theologians, "Let's drink to
the fact that at last we have an existentially viable her-
meneutic!"). No, when Jesus has vanished, the episode is
finished. Truth cannot be clutched and coddled, the story tells
us. The action must continue. Like Jesus, they must go elsewhere. They must go and tell people what has happened.

And so, having scarcely completed the seven-mile hike from
Jerusalem to Emmaus, the disciples have to turn around and go
back from Emmaus to Jerusalem, another seven-mile hike, and
tell the story of what has happened. The road to Emmaus, it
turns out, does not lead to Emmaus but back to Jerusalem—
from the scene of the *action,* through the *reflection,* to a new
kind of *action,* action in the midst of the fear and anxiety and
danger they had left just a few hours earlier, but action now

undergirded by new understanding that can deal with the fear and the anxiety, if not the danger.

So at the end of the story they are right back where they started, but now everything is different. Before, they were behind locked doors, saving their necks. Now they are about to start going out all over the Roman Empire, putting their necks on the line every day. That action, once begun, has no terminus.

OTHER BIBLICAL PASSAGES

The Fourth Gospel gives us more help on this new relationship between knowing and doing. Jesus is in Jerusalem, engaging in the presumptuous activity of teaching within the Temple. Presumptuous, indeed, because he's a nobody from out of town. The people he is addressing—well-educated university degree holders, many of whom have done graduate work—are puzzled by the fact that a nobody from out of town can be so wise when he never finished high school, let alone spent four years at a good Ivy League college.

"How is it," they ask themselves, "that this man has learning when he has never studied?" (John 7:15).

Jesus, overhearing their question, continues to deserve the adjective "presumptuous." "My teaching," he informs them, "is not mine, but [God's] who sent me."

This is not enough for the skeptics. They want credentials: degrees, a *curriculum vitae,* membership in learned societies, a list of recent publications. "What a claim!" they must have muttered under their breath, and "How are we expected to believe *that?*"—as Jesus goes on, "If anyone's will is to *do* God's will, that one shall *know* whether the teaching is from God or whether I am speaking on my own authority" (John 7:15–17, italics added).

A little later, Jesus puts the capstone on the argument by

saying to another group, not scoffers this time but believers, "If you continue in my word [i.e., doing what is asked of you], you are truly my disciples, and you will know the truth, and the truth will make you free" (John 8:31–32).

The connected episodes illustrate what the Fourth Gospel elsewhere calls "doing the truth" (John 3:21)—not knowing, or perceiving, or intuiting the truth but "doing" the truth.

Is the teaching true? Jesus replies to the scoffers, "Try living it; that's the only way you'll ever find out," while to believers he says, "Keep on living it and you will be set free, liberated. That will be the sign of its truth for you."

Like the scoffers, we would appreciate demonstrations: "Prove to us that you are right. Mount an intellectual argument that will convince us. Provide enough data so that we can take you seriously." And, like the believers, we would prefer the truth on less exacting terms: "Can't we just settle for intellectual assent? Why all the fuss about 'doing'? That's a whole other ball game."

But it's not another ball game, Jesus is saying in effect, it's the only game in town. He is simply asserting what his followers on the road to Emmaus also discovered, that only in the midst of commitment, of *doing* the truth, will we ever discover its truth for us. After that, if we wish, there will be plenty of time to theologize.

How unfortunate! No proofs ahead of time. No gateway to knowledge except one marked "Risk."

ITEMS FOR REFLECTION AND DISCUSSION

1. Many third world Christians talk about a "hermeneutical circle," which, in rough translation, means a circle of interpretation; that is to say, how we interpret our experience, our world, our Scriptures, our selves, in ways that avoid "distancing" ourselves and separating knowing and doing. Here is a modified hermeneutical circle based on the Emmaus story:

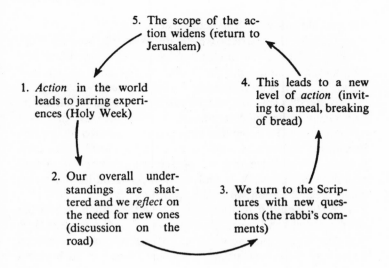

5. The scope of the action widens (return to Jerusalem)

1. *Action* in the world leads to jarring experiences (Holy Week)

4. This leads to a new level of *action* (inviting to a meal, breaking of bread)

2. Our overall understandings are shattered and we *reflect* on the need for new ones (discussion on the road)

3. We turn to the Scriptures with new questions (the rabbi's comments)

The process begins all over again as the disciples leave Jerusalem to go "to all nations" (Luke 24:47) and have new "jarring experiences."

How adaptable is this to our own situation? What promise does it hold? What are the threats?

2. The philosopher George Santayana once wrote that those who ignore history are doomed to repeat it. How similar is this to what the rabbi told the confused disciples about needing to understand the past in order to understand the present? Test it against the following: *(a)* If we "forget Vietnam," we are likely to repeat its mistakes elsewhere, *(b)* If we forget the Holocaust against the Jews in the 1930s and 1940s, we are likely to repeat it in nuclear terms against Jews and everyone else in the 1980s or 1990s. To put it another way: If we want to understand the way in which rich nations exploit poor nations today, we have to know something about the history of colonialism and how past exploitation is repeated today under

different slogans and in new disguises.

3. Explore the barriers we create to avoid the leap from thinking to doing. To discuss "redemption" is one thing and might even be the topic for a seminar; to have to act in a redeeming way is quite another matter. To have a theology of "forgiveness" is splendid; actually to have to forgive that miserable person who tried to muscle in on a business deal is a different story. To know that the poor are exploited by the rich in Central America is a social fact we can handle and even lament; to recognize that we ourselves are complicit in that exploitation, financing it and supporting it militarily, raises challenges for action we would rather not face.

4. What would it really mean to take the fourth step in the story seriously and share the truth we have? If a student does that during an examination, it's called cheating; maybe we need a new way of testing learning. If someone does it in the business world, it's called a sure road to bankruptcy; maybe we need a new way of organizing our economic life. If we do it with our religious convictions, our friends are likely to think we are off our rockers; maybe we need a new understanding of what things are really important.

2. EXODUS:
GOD TAKES SIDES
(Changing Sides)

Exodus 1:8–14; 2:23–25; 3:7–10

We have been brought up to believe in a God who is the God of *all* people—rich, poor, white, black, Asian, African, North American, South American. We are perturbed when we read that the belt buckles of German soldiers in World War I had the words *Gott mit uns* (God with us) inscribed on them, as though God were supporting the Germans rather than the French, Belgians, English, and Americans. We ought to be equally perturbed when our own political leaders equate the cause of America with the cause of God, pitting us against a "godless" foe, the very "focus of evil."

The notion of God exercising indiscriminate love toward all is a healthy protection against racists, who do not believe God really loves dark-skinned peoples, or against North Americans who instinctively feel (even when they deny it) that God is more concerned about them than about the unemployed workers who flock to Mexico City every day.

And yet there is something false and unbiblical about this view of God's relationship to the world's peoples, as we can see if we pit *other* groups against each other and ask whether God is equally their God. Is God as much the God of the torturers as the God of the tortured? Is God equally the God of the military dictator and the God of those who are murdered by the dictator? Does God have the same disposition toward the victim of a plant closedown in Akron, Ohio, as toward members of the

Board of Directors who shut down the plant with no concern for what will happen to the workers?

Our conventional God is aloof from such things; any other God would be a partisan God—worse yet, a "political" God— taking sides with some of God's children and against others. And that is hard for us to swallow.

But it is not hard for the biblical writers to swallow. Indeed, they affirm such a God strongly. We will look at one passage, the story of the exodus, that describes a very partisan God who takes sides with a vengeance. If it were only an isolated passage, we could dispose of it, but it has set its stamp on the whole Bible and has become a paradigm passage for third world Christians living in situations of oppression and injustice similar to the Egyptian situation. To fail to take it seriously is to fail to take the Bible seriously.

THE BIBLICAL TEXT: EXODUS 1:8–14; 2:23–25; 3:7–10

[8]Now there arose a new king over Egypt, who did not know Joseph. [9]And he said to his people, "Behold, the people of Israel are too many and too mighty for us. [10]Come, let us deal shrewdly with them, lest they multiply, and, if war befall us, they join our enemies and fight against us and escape from the land." [11]Therefore they set taskmasters over them to afflict them with heavy burdens; and they built for Pharaoh store cities, Pithom and Raamses. [12]But the more they were oppressed, the more they multiplied and the more they spread abroad. And the Egyptians were in dread of the people of Israel. [13]So they made the people of Israel serve with rigor, [14]and made their lives bitter with hard service, in mortar and brick, and in all kinds of work in the field; in all their work they made them serve with rigor.

[2:23]In the course of those many days the king of Egypt died. And the people of Israel groaned under their bondage, and cried out for help, and their cry under bondage came up to God. ²⁴And God heard their groaning, and God remembered his covenant with Abraham, with Isaac, and with Jacob. ²⁵And God saw the people of Israel, and God knew their condition.

3:7Then the LORD said, "I have seen the affliction of my people who are in Egypt, and have heard their cry because of their taskmasters; I know their sufferings, ⁸and I have come down to deliver them out of the hand of the Egyptians, and to bring them up out of that land to a good and broad land, a land flowing with milk and honey. . . .

⁹And now, behold, the cry of the people of Israel has come to me, and I have seen the oppression with which the Egyptians oppress them. ¹⁰Come, I will send you to Pharaoh that you may bring forth my people, the sons of Israel, out of Egypt."

The above passages are snippets of a story that extends over fifteen chapters of Exodus (if one wants to be concise) and over the whole of the Bible (if one wants to be precise). Even in these few verses, however, the main outlines of the story are clear:

1. A class struggle is going on.
2. God is aware of the struggle.
3. God takes sides in the struggle.
4. God calls people to join in the struggle.

We start with the people. And what is happening to the people? The first passage above makes clear that *a class struggle is going on.*

It would be easy for us to digest that claim if only the word "class" were omitted; who could disagree that a "struggle" is going on? But the term "class struggle" has been used deliberately; in the modern world, Christians need to do more than bristle when they hear the words "class struggle." For although

Karl Marx may have invented the term, he didn't invent the reality; he merely noticed it and called it to the attention of others. If there is any situation to which it applies, surely the situation described in our text qualifies: it is a story of masters and slaves, kings and chattel, oppressors and oppressed, owners and workers. There are two *classes* of people involved, and they are locked in *struggle.* To reject the term is to reject the story.

It's a pretty uneven struggle. The Israelites are slaves, the king and his crowd are slaveowners. One side holds all the trump cards and aces. If that sounds like a stacked deck, nobody should be surprised, for when one class can make the lives of the other class "bitter with hard service, in mortar and brick and in all kinds of work" (Ex. 1:14), the deck *is* stacked.

Here, then, is a classic oppressor/oppressed situation, complete with intimidation, humiliation, forced labor, powerlessness, and genocide. When the slaves ask for a three-day weekend to go off and worship God, the king's response is typical of how oppressors everywhere respond: he not only doesn't grant requests but makes things even worse than before—*that* will teach them. So Pharaoh tells the taskmasters that not only must the slaves continue to make as many bricks per day as they did before, but from now on, rather than having straw provided for them, they must provide it themselves. After all, if they have time to go off and worship some god, they obviously aren't being worked hard enough.

What happens in such situations is that the oppressed "internalize their oppression"; that is to say, they accept their lowly status as appropriate or inevitable and, believing themselves powerless to produce change, lose hope. All this happens to the Israelites. They become so shattered that when Moses offers an agenda for protest, "they [do] not listen to Moses, because of their broken spirit and their cruel bondage" (Ex. 6:9).

After the first passage cited above comes a story about midwives, to whom we shall return. There is also a story about a young man named Moses, to whom we shall likewise return: the

child of a slave, he grows up, kills an Egyptian taskmaster, and
flees to Midian until it is time for him to enter stage left.

In the second passage, the story moves from the sociological
account of a struggle in which one side holds all the cards to the
theological assertion that *God is aware of the struggle*—the same
God who had previously entered into a "covenant" or special
agreement with the folks who presently hold none of the cards.

Things have gotten so bad that the Israelites cry out to God.
They need help, and they need it badly, and they need it right
away. And the good news is that God is not exclusively wrapped
up in contemplation of divine attributes but is aware of the
Israelites' plight; God realizes that certain covenantal agreements already referred to make it necessary for something to
happen.

It is through Moses' encounter with God in the wilderness
that we learn, in the third passage, that something *is* going to
happen. Not only is God "aware," which might be consoling
without necessarily changing things, but Moses is told that *God
takes sides in the struggle,* which introduces fantastic new pos-
sibilities for whichever side is favored with divine assistance.
And, as is the consistent pattern throughout the Bible, God does
not side with the powerful, the friends of Pharaoh who think
they hold history in the palms of their hands, but with the slaves,
who up to this moment have had nothing in the palms of their
hands but calluses.

God's promise is double-edged: not only liberation *from*
Egypt but liberation *for* the Promised Land. "I know their
sufferings," God informs Moses, "and I have come down to
deliver them out of the hand of the Egyptians, and to bring them
up out of that land to a good and broad land" (Ex. 3:7–8). God
promises *political* liberation (the only kind that would count)
from the economic and social bondage Israel had endured. Despite what some of God's later emissaries may have reported,
God believes that religion and politics mix.

There is more to come. All of the above could be a recipe for

passivity, an invitation to wait for God to move into high gear
and take over—which is not the way God operates. For the God
who has just said "*I* have come down to deliver them out of the
hand of the Egyptians" follows up by saying to Moses, "Come,
I will send *you* to Pharaoh that *you* may bring forth my people"
(Ex. 3:10, italics added). *God calls people to join in the struggle.*
Moses will be God's emissary to Pharaoh, the one through
whom, along with the other Israelites, God's determination to
liberate them will actually be accomplished. The people, trust-
ing in the power of the Lord, are to be *the vehicles of their own
liberation.* God will not do it without their help. They must act
on their own behalf.

God, while intervening on behalf of the weak, is quite prepared to use the weak. Moses, to offer a brilliant example, is as
weak as they come; he ducks and weaves in every possible way
to avoid the body blow of an assignment, piling up excuses
ranging from the fact that he doesn't know God's name to the
fact that he stutters and would therefore be a singularly ineffec-
tive negotiator with Pharaoh. No matter, God can use even such
unpromising material—a consoling thought for the rest of us.

A beautiful example of God's enlisting the people in their own
struggle occurs earlier in the account (Ex. 1:15–22), demonstrat-
ing that the real heroes of the liberation are actually heroines—a
fact our male-dominated scriptures usually cover up. Fearful of a
population increase among the Israelites, Pharaoh instructs the
Hebrew midwives to kill the sons of any Hebrew women at whose
births they are assisting. The midwives ignore the king's instructions. Sometime later, having seen no notable diminution in the
number of Hebrew males on the streets of the royal city, Pharaoh
summons the midwives and demands an accounting. The midwives, who are canny, beat him at his own game. They tell him
that Hebrew women are more vigorous and in better shape than
Egyptian women and always seem to have delivered their own
babies, without help, by the time the midwives get there.

While this may be a blow to the midwives' incomes, it is a

great boon to the Israelite birthrate, and as a result "the people multiplied and grew very strong" (Ex. 1:20), which was one of God's ways of preparing them to share in the liberation struggle. But God couldn't have done it without the midwives.

We have seen enough to secure the main lines of the exodus story: in a situation of oppression . . . God takes sides . . . with the oppressed . . . to free them from oppression . . . by empowering them to share in the liberation struggle. The rest is footnotes.

OTHER BIBLICAL PASSAGES

This time we are going to cheat a little. Instead of pointing to a variety of passages as elaborations of the exodus story, we will suggest that this story is so pivotal that the rest of the Bible is commentary on it. When Latin American Christians are accused of putting too much stress on the exodus narrative, Gustavo Gutiérrez rightly responds that the exodus narrative is only a vivid example of the biblical narrative as a whole, a narrative that has as its central theme "liberation for the oppressed."

Throughout the rest of this book, therefore, readers are urged to see how the various passages corroborate themes of the story we are now examining. An excellent third world resource for this task is Croatto, *Exodus: A Hermeneutics of Freedom,* which elaborates not only the exodus story itself but also its influence on the Genesis creation stories, the message of the prophets, the mission of Jesus, and the writings of Paul.

ITEMS FOR REFLECTION AND DISCUSSION

The text confronts us with three questions: (1) How do third world Christians hear this passage? (2) How do we hear it? and (3) How can we deal with the differences?

1. *How do third world Christians hear this passage?* Their bottom line is that since God is a living God, the story is not

only a historical account of God's liberating activity back then but also an ongoing account of God's liberating activity today.

Third world Christians do not need Karl Marx to realize that *a class struggle is going on.* Knowing that they are oppressed is not something gleaned from books; it is gnawing hunger in the gut, family members taken off at 2 A.M. to face torture and death, children growing up so malnourished that permanent brain damage results, and the realization that 80 percent of their people live in unredeemed poverty while the rest live in unimagined opulence.

It is not hard for them to figure out who the oppressors are. They are the little handful on top who have the wealth and power—meaning guns, tanks, and torture chambers—to stay on top and keep the rest on the bottom.

As they reflect on this situation, third world Christians go a step further. They see that the modern pharaohs couldn't continue in power without help from outside, and they see much of that help coming from the United States of America—help that enabled the Somoza family to maintain dictatorial control of Nicaragua for forty years, that has kept Pinochet in dictatorial control of Chile for ten years, that has continuously legitimized Marcos' dictatorial control of the Philippines and that has supported innumerable dictatorial juntas in El Salvador and Guatemala. They see the United States consistently supporting dictators all over the world—wherever it is in its own political and economic self-interest to do so—regardless of what that means for the victims of dictatorial rule.

But there is good news. They are not alone. *God is aware of the struggle* they face. They, too, groan under their bondage and cry out for help (Ex. 2:23). And they, too, believe that God sees them and knows their condition (Ex. 2:25). When the Brazilian bishops issue a pastoral letter about injustice in their land, they use as their title God's declaration "I have heard the cry of my people." The Spanish word for "cry" is *el grito,* which means "scream" and conveys more clearly the immensity of their plight.

There is even better news: God is not only a listening God but a responding God who acts. The source of hope for third world Christians is that *God takes sides in the struggle* and that God takes *their* side. If that sounds like a relic of the *Gott mit uns* mentality, put it another way: God always sides with the oppressed, and it is among the oppressed that most third world Christians happen to be. A God siding with the tyrants would be a God of malevolence; a God siding with no one would appear to be a God of indifference but would also be a God of malevolence, giving support to the tyrants by not opposing them; only a God siding with the oppressed would be a God of justice, a God worthy of the name.

The best news of all is that Christians can participate in throwing off oppression, for *God calls them to join in the struggle.* They need not remain helpless and powerless. God empowers them to do something about their situation. They know from centuries of experience that the oppressors will not voluntarily relinquish power. They know that if another nation "helps" them defeat the oppressor, that nation will become their new oppressor. So they see that they must achieve their own liberation, and that this is what God wants for them. Nourished by such faith, they struggle to challenge the oppressors, organizing resistance movements and working in every way possible to ensure that their children will have enough to eat and can go to bed without fear.

2. *How do we hear the exodus story?* If such a response to the exodus story is even close to target, it puts the rest of us in quite a bind. But if we are to be honest with the biblical materials, we cannot ignore such a reading. Let us go through the sequence again and see what it says to us.

We are likely to resist the notion that *a class struggle is going on,* for at least three reasons: (1) because we have been programmed to believe that anything that "sounds Marxist" is wrong; (2) because we doubt that in our complex world the distinctions between oppressors and oppressed can be so neatly drawn; and (3) because if the distinctions hold, we end up among the oppressors, and we don't think that's fair. Who among us gets up in the morning asking, "Let's see, who can I oppress today?"

So let us hear how third world Christians press the case. Put yourself, they might say, in the shoes of a Chilean woman living in Santiago in 1973. The Allende government, democratically elected, is politically "leftist." But there is milk for the woman's children, and the economy, while precarious, is not as skewed in favor of the rich as before. She has hope for the future, believing that Chile can be governed for the benefit of all and not just the rich.

And then, in early September, the army appears in the streets, bombs the government buildings, assassinates the president, and institutes martial law under General Pinochet. His military dictatorship entrenches itself in power. Inflation rises at a staggering rate. Her husband, along with thousands of others, is seized, interrogated, and tortured and is never seen again. In January she is informed that she can claim his body in the city morgue; it seems he fell and injured himself while exercising in the jail yard. She herself is picked up for questioning and is detained in prison for six weeks, during which time she is unable to make contact with her children, the oldest of whom also "disappears," which is a polite way of saying that the government has murdered him for alleged support of the previous regime.

After her release, the Chilean woman discovers that American business groups had developed elaborate plans to "destabilize" the Chilean economy under Allende so that there would be a pretext for the U.S.-supported military takeover by Pinochet; that the American President and Secretary of State had supported plans for the overthrow (the Secretary of State having said, "Why should we let Chile go communist just because the Chileans don't know any better?"); that many of the Chilean torturers had been trained in American police academies in Panama and Washington; and that it had been a fixed item of

State Department policy that Chile should be prevented from consolidating a "socialist" government.

Given these circumstances, our third world friends would ask us, is it any wonder that the Chilean woman counts not only the Chilean junta but the American government among the "oppressors" of her people? Is there not truly a class struggle going on today, just as there was in Egypt? And which side, they would continue to press, are you on?

The notion of class struggle is so difficult for us that the second notion, that *God is aware of the struggle,* may be easier to take hold of initially. We can affirm that God is aware of what is going on in God's world, and while we may not think God sees it the way the Chilean woman sees it, the fact that God *does see* is a given.

We might not even have difficulty with the notion that *God takes sides in the struggle*—until we have to determine *which* side God takes. Our own preference, of course, would be to have God take sides with Pharaoh (read Pinochet) in such a way as to enlighten Pharaoh, bring about a change in Pharaoh's heart, inspire Pharaoh to create better working conditions for the slaves, persuade Pharaoh to give them a three-day weekend (maybe even once a month), and have Pharaoh see to it that the overseers stop treating the slaves so brutally. That would delight us, not least because *it would not upset the existing structures of society at all;* it would just "humanize" them a bit.

But unfortunately, the biblical writers didn't consult us. All they say about Pharaoh's heart is that God "hardened" it rather than enlightening it, which will have to remain a theological problem for another occasion, since the important thing at the moment is to notice that *God does not enlighten the powerful but empowers the powerless.*

That is very good news to the powerless.

And it is very bad news to the powerful—which is the part of the story we've got to confront, for it is pretty clear that where we fit in the exodus story is among the functionaries in Pharaoh's court rather than among the workers in the slave labor camps. We don't make the big political decisions, but we acquiesce in them; we don't torture people, but our tax money supports the training of torturers; we don't force dictators on the Chileans, but we are complicit in our government's decision to do so. We end up, almost by default, among the oppressors. And if God takes sides with the oppressed, God must also be taking sides against the oppressors. Against us. Bad news.

There's a further affirmation: *God calls people to join in the struggle.* Stated that way, the claim seems reasonable; no one has a right to sit on his or her hands and wait for God to do the work. But in Exodus the claim is that *God empowers the oppressed to work for their liberation,* and that means overthrowing the oppressors. Servants in Pharaoh's court are not going to fare too well in the light of such an agenda.

3. So, to come to our final question, *how can we deal with the differences between these readings of the story?*

If we are going to try, it means starting with an acknowledgment that the third world version of the story is closer to the biblical version than is our own. And if that is so, we are on the wrong side of the struggle. *Is it possible to change sides?* That question will be central for the rest of this book. Here we can only begin an answer.

Dom Helder Câmara, the archbishop of Recife, Brazil—which is perhaps the poorest area in the whole of South America—once said to a group of visiting North Americans, "If you are appalled by what you see here, please don't try to start a revolution for us—a revolution from which you can flee when real bullets start flying. If you really want to help us, go back to your own country and work to change the policies of your government that exploit our country and keep our people so poor."

We cannot be other than who we are—North Americans who are part of a vast complex of military and economic and political power. But we have an advantage: political and social structures are available to us through which we can work to move that

power in less exploitive directions. Both Reinhold Niebuhr and
Pope Paul VI (otherwise unlikely theological companions) gave
a pointer for that endeavor: If you want peace, they said, work
for justice. In the light of the exodus story that means, first of
all, refusing any longer to be compliant members of Pharaoh's
court and instead using our positions within the court to challenge Pharaoh's policies. That is a tall order.

But sometimes, probably most times, Pharaoh won't budge.
And at such times it is no longer enough to try to reform
Pharaoh. One has to break with Pharaoh. Instead of changing
Pharaoh, one has to change sides. That is the tallest order of all,
but fortunately it is also very biblical, and we will examine many
examples of doing it in the following pages. As an initial pointer,
consider the experiences of the Latin American bishops.

For centuries, the Catholic Church in Latin America was on
the side of Pharaoh. It told the poor to be patient and accept
present earthly misery in exchange for anticipated heavenly
treasure. It told the poor not to rock the boat, not to challenge
structures, not to organize, not to form unions. The rich loved
it.

And then something began to happen to the bishops. Some
of them overheard Jesus in the synagogue in Nazareth talking
about "good news to the poor" (see Chapter 6) and began to
realize that he really meant it. Others became more aware of the
poor in their midst than they had been before. And so gradually,
but with increasing conviction, they began to be advocates for
the poor and to challenge political and economic structures that
kept the poor powerless.

The rich decided this was dirty pool. "You're taking sides,"
they accused the bishops. "Religion and politics don't mix." To
which the bishops could only respond, "You've got it all wrong.
For centuries we took *your* side, and you never complained
about that particular mix of religion and politics. No, it's not the
case that we have started 'taking sides.' We are merely changing
sides."

POSTSCRIPT: AN IMMEDIATE WARNING
AND AN ULTIMATE HOPE

In the rest of the exodus story, the Israelites not only make
it out of Egypt but even (after a discouraging forty-year delay
in the desert) make it into the Promised Land. Once there, they
give the displaced inhabitants a rough time. The *nouveaux riches*
pile up more wealth for themselves, and the widows and or-
phans—the most defenseless and powerless members of society
—become favorite targets for easy exploitation. As one contemporary report describes the scene, "[The rich] have devoured
human lives; they have taken treasure and precious things; they
have made many widows in the midst of [the land]." The oppressed, once they have gained power, become oppressors.

The story has a dreary familiarity to all who have studied
social transformation. The names and numbers of the players
change, but the nature of the game does not; broad-based social
movements, born of idealism and selfless commitment, harden
into tightly knit oligarchies nurtured by cynicism and self-
aggrandizement. The last state is no better, and is often worse,
than the first.

This reality becomes a justification for those who want to
stick with the status quo. "Why seek change?" they argue. "The
new regime will be just as bad as the old one."

The appeal of the argument, of course, is limited to those
already on top. They want to stay on top and reap the benefits
of their privileged position; if they are clever and calculating
enough, they will toss just enough crumbs to the poor to prevent
social upheaval. They use words like "stability" and "law and
order" to justify putting down any attempts at change. Pharaoh's court was full of such persons. It still is.

Those at the bottom see the specious nature of such argu-
ments. And when things get bad enough to mount significant
movements for change, they have at least two fallback argu-

ments: (1) nothing could be worse than the way things are now, so *any* change would be a change for the better; and anyhow, (2) *this* time it's going to be different, because we are not going to make the mistake of becoming carbon copies of the tyrants we replace.

As far as the first argument goes, nobody who is eating well has the privilege of telling starving people that things aren't as bad as they think; the rest of us have a moral obligation to take them at their word.

As far as the second argument goes, the Bible has at least two important things to say. First, it tells us that because God is just, there is a moral dimension to history, so that those who act oppressively—both present tyrants and those who overthrow them and become tyrants themselves—will be brought down and destroyed in the long run.

The answer to that argument is that long-run answers, while consoling, don't help much in the short run. As John Maynard Keynes observed, "In the long run we'll all be dead." So there is a second biblical answer: The best way to keep the oppressed from becoming oppressors is by ongoing protest *from within* the liberation movements. The description in the first paragraph of this postscript, of Israel's oppressive conduct in the Promised Land, is not an outsider's attempt to score points against Jews but is part of the biblical book of Ezekiel (22:25).

The story of Amos is a vivid illustration of the same point. Amos, the farm boy from Tekoa, comes down to the big city of Bethel. He is appalled by the graft, corruption, and exploitation. So he goes to Hyde Park Corner, mounts his soapbox, and does a very clever thing. First of all, he endears himself to his hearers by ticking off the sins of all of Israel's enemies—Damascus, Gaza, Tyre, Edom, Ammon, Moab, and Judah. The crowd loves him. What prophetic fervor! What perception about the sins of our enemies! What insight about their abuses of power! How splendidly reassuring to hear that God is going to destroy them all!

But their satisfaction is short-lived. Amos punctures his hearers' complacency by turning his sharp words against the folk in Bethel itself: Unless the Israelites repent, they too will be destroyed. Why? Because "they sell the righteous for silver, and the needy for a pair of shoes—they . . . trample the head of the poor into the dust of the earth, and turn aside the way of the afflicted" (Amos 2:6–7)—which is a handy summary of exactly what Pharaoh did to those same Israelites in Egypt, save that this time the sandal is on the other foot.

Amos did not win the Boy Orator of the Year Award from the Bethel Chamber of Commerce, despite the fact that he surely spoke with a clear, well-modulated voice. But his devastating indictment is not preserved within the writings of the Jews' enemies; it is preserved within the sacred writings of the Jews themselves.

Amos is one of dozens of voices—all recorded within the Jewish Scriptures—who *from within the life of Israel* keep exhorting Israel not to forsake its commitment to justice, and who keep calling attention to every miscarriage of justice. Commitment to Yahweh, the God of justice, always carries the potential for correcting injustice and saves the biblical demand for radical change from the accusation of the cynics that the oppressed inevitably become oppressors.

Our next two chapters will carry the theme forward as we examine how Nathan and Jeremiah, two more prophets, challenge the policies of kings and help formerly oppressed people avoid becoming instruments of new oppression.

3. DAVID AND NATHAN:
CHALLENGING THE ABUSE OF POWER
(Changing Stories)

2 Samuel 11:2–17, 26–27; 12:1–7

We are living in a time of intense nationalism. Precisely at the moment in history when we must become one human family or destroy ourselves, the leaders of the major powers seem determined to set us at enmity with one another. Russian leaders describe all nations who are not their satellites, and especially the United States, as "imperialist capitalist warmongers" out to gain economic control of the entire globe for their own ends. Our leaders describe left-wing nations, and especially the Soviet Union, as "godless atheists" (a curious linguistic redundancy) out to gain political control of the entire globe for their own ends. The implication of the rhetoric of both sides is clear: purity resides with us, evil is located elsewhere, and we can pinpoint its location exactly, if you really want to know.

But the problem is not just our leaders. The problem is ourselves. We, too, adopt this way of thinking and (whether we use the phrase or not) affirm the toast of Stephen Decatur, "Our country! . . . may she always be in the right; but our country, right or wrong." The world would be fine, we assert, if it weren't for all those "other" countries that threaten our security, or chant "Yankee, go home!", or elect "socialist" leaders, or protest against our locating missile sites within their boundaries. If only they would realize that whatever we are doing is for their own good. . . .

Most of such talk is open and aboveboard, clear and unambiguous. There are few rhetorical inhibitions these days when it comes to extolling our own virtues and drawing attention to someone else's vices. But there is another attitude that is even more threatening. It implies that criticism of one's own country (or one's own point of view, or one's own church) is hitting below the belt and therefore against the rules. To criticize, particularly in a public way, is to weaken the cause of those criticized; it thus becomes an act of disloyalty that gives aid and comfort to the enemy. "America—Love It or Leave It" really means "To love America is *not* to criticize it, and if you criticize it you *ought* to leave it and go to Russia, since you've already indicated that's where your true allegiance lies."

There is a biblical story that challenges this way of thinking. It insists that loyalty to a country or a leader should never be uncritical loyalty and that sometimes, in the interest of truth, criticism is not only justifiable but morally necessary. We might call it the Nathan syndrome.

THE BIBLICAL TEXT: 2 SAMUEL 11:2–17, 26–27; 12:1–7

²It happened, late one afternoon, when David arose from his couch and was walking upon the roof of the king's house, that he saw from the roof a woman bathing; and the woman was very beautiful. ³And David sent and inquired about the woman. And one said, "Is not this Bathsheba, the daughter of Eliam, the wife of Uriah the Hittite?" ⁴So David sent messengers, and took her; and she came to him, and he lay with her. (Now she was purifying herself from her uncleanness.) Then she returned to her house. ⁵And the woman conceived; and she sent and told David, "I am with child."

⁶So David sent word to Joab, "Send me Uriah the Hittite." And Joab sent Uriah to David. ⁷When Uriah came to him, David asked how Joab was doing, and how the people fared, and how the war prospered. ⁸Then David said to Uriah, "Go down to your house, and wash your

feet." And Uriah went out of the king's house, and there followed him a present from the king. ⁹But Uriah slept at the door of the king's house with all the servants of his lord, and did not go down to his house. ¹⁰When they told David, "Uriah did not go down to his house," David said to Uriah, "Have you not come from a journey? Why did you not go down to your house?" ¹¹Uriah said to David, "The ark and Israel and Judah dwell in booths; and my lord Joab and the servants of my lord are camping in the open field; shall I then go to my house, to eat and to drink, and to lie with my wife? As you live, and as your soul lives, I will not do this thing." ¹²Then David said to Uriah, "Remain here today also, and tomorrow I will let you depart." So Uriah remained in Jerusalem that day, and the next. ¹³And David invited him, and he ate in his presence and drank, so that he made him drunk; and in the evening he went out to lie on his couch with the servants of his lord, but he did not go down to his house.

¹⁴In the morning David wrote a letter to Joab, and sent it by the hand of Uriah. ¹⁵In the letter he wrote, "Set Uriah in the forefront of the hardest fighting, and then draw back from him, that he may be struck down, and die." ¹⁶And as Joab was besieging the city, he assigned Uriah to the place where he knew there were valiant men. ¹⁷And the men of the city came out and fought with Joab; and some of the servants of David among the people fell. Uriah the Hittite was slain also. . . .

²⁶When the wife of Uriah heard that Uriah her husband was dead, she made lamentation for her husband. ²⁷And when the mourning was over, David sent and brought her to his house, and she became his wife, and bore him a son. But the thing that David had done displeased the LORD.

¹²:¹And the LORD sent Nathan to David. He came to him, and said to him, "There were two men in a certain city, the one rich and the other poor. ²The rich man had very many flocks and herds; ³but the poor man had nothing but one little ewe lamb, which he had bought. And he

brought it up, and it grew up with him and with his
children; it used to eat of his morsel, and drink from his
cup, and lie in his bosom, and it was like a daughter to
him. 'Now there came a traveler to the rich man, and he
was unwilling to take one of his own flock or herd to
prepare for the wayfarer who had come to him, but he
took the poor man's lamb, and prepared it for the man
who had come to him." ⁵Then David's anger was greatly
kindled against the man; and he said to Nathan, "As the
LORD lives, the man who has done this deserves to die;
⁶and he shall restore the lamb fourfold, because he did this
thing, and because he had no pity."
    ⁷Nathan said to David, "You are the man."

The story is actually three stories. First, it is the story of
David and his adulterous relationship with Bathsheba—which
is the way most comfortably situated people read it. To us it is
a message of moral judgment, telling us that adultery is wrong
and that it leads to things like deception and murder. Second,
it is the story of Nathan and his stern relationship with David
—which is the way most oppressed people suffering under evil
tyrants read it. To them it is a message of hope, indicating that
it is possible to stand up to those who abuse power, and to say
no. Third, it is the story of a ewe lamb—an apparently innocent
little fable that ties the other two stories together.

    1. *The David Story* is a highly moral tale of the private and
public consequences of personal iniquity. Although the language of our translations is a little coy, it doesn't take much
imagination to see what's happening.

    King David is at home in the palace while the troops are off
in the hills doing battle. One afternoon he sees a woman, Bathsheba, sunbathing in the nude and wants to have sex with her.
A predictable regal sequence follows in two steps: (1) king
desires woman; (2) king gets woman. Only this time there is a
third step: (3) king gets woman pregnant.

What to do? The woman, to complicate matters, has a husband, Uriah. To complicate matters further, he is out of town, off with the troops loyally fighting the Ammonites for the king. David, who puts great store on appearances, cooks up a scheme. Out of his thoughtfulness for the needs of his fighting men, he will recall Uriah from the front lines for a period of rest and recreation at home. Uriah, of course, will sleep with Bathsheba, and when word is sent to the front a few days later that she is pregnant, Uriah will assume joyfully and without further thought that the child to be born is his own. End of problem for King David.

A clever scheme that has only one flaw. Uriah will not cooperate. A man of ultrasensitive conscience, he does not feel entitled to court Bathsheba while his army buddies in Charlie Company are courting death. So he does not spend the night in bed with his wife after all.

David, well acquainted with what military men do on leave, has hardly expected loyalty to military comrades to outweigh the charms of Bathsheba. So he extends Uriah's leave for another day (and night). The fallback plan seems foolproof: he will ply Uriah with the king's best wines, and Uriah, after a sufficient number of rounds, will find his conscience so numbed and his libido so aroused that he will race home from the royal banquet to have sex not once but twice before returning to battle. But once again, Uriah, conscious of the plight of his less fortunate comrades-in-arms, spends the night not in his wife's arms but in the servant's quarters.

David is desperate. He knows that anybody like Uriah who can count up to nine is going to figure out that the baby is not his. So, in desperation, David sends Uriah back to the front lines with a sealed envelope for his commander, a sealed envelope that contains Uriah's death warrant. Joab, the recipient of the sealed envelope and Uriah's superior officer, is instructed to see to it that Uriah dies in battle. Whatever Joab may think of the instructions, he knows, good military man that he is, that "orders are orders" and that the head of state is also commander in chief of the armed forces. His battle plan contains provision for Uriah to be killed by the Ammonites. Word is relayed back to the palace. The commander in chief of the armed forces generously forgives Major Joab for the clumsy military maneuver that cost the life of his valiant Sergeant Uriah, and Sergeant Uriah is buried with full military honors and posthumously given the Legion of Valor medal. The king himself attends the funeral. After the prescribed period of mourning for her dead husband, Bathsheba moves into the palace, there is a betrothal ceremony, and—a trifle prematurely to be sure—a son is born to the happy royal couple. End of 2 Samuel, chapter 11.

2. The David Story might have ended here, everything tidily back in place, had it not been for *The Nathan Story,* which begins with 2 Samuel, chapter 12. We know a lot less about Nathan than we do about David, but we know enough (cf. 2 Sam. 7:1–17) to form some preliminary assessment of him before we meet him here.

Nathan is one of the prophets in the king's court, which means that when the king has to make decisions, the retinue of prophets is supposed, by various means at its disposal, to inform the king of God's will. Any king with any sense will take his prophets seriously, for he would much prefer to have God on his side rather than on someone else's.

Sometimes there is a conflict. Once, for example, David had wanted to build a temple to the Lord, and Nathan, responding to what he was told by the Lord, went out on a limb and indicated that David was not—repeat not—to build a temple to the Lord. This took considerable courage on Nathan's part, not only because Nathan, in reporting God's will, was ranging himself against David's will—which is an uncomfortable position for a prophet to be in—but also because he had previously been part of the pro-temple crowd, urging David to go ahead with his construction plans, until the latest revelation from Yahweh forced a change in the message, which he now had to communicate in his official prophetic status.

So Nathan, when we meet him in chapter 12, is not just some outsider who can stride onstage, deliver a blistering attack as the punch line to bring down the curtain on Act II, and leave forever. No, he has been onstage all the time, part of the royal household, a member of the inner circle. And those who challenge the inner circle are often invited to accept one-way tickets to the outer circle.

At the time we pick up the story, Nathan has survived that earlier crossing of the regal will, so he already has a bit of a track record in saying no to the king, although such an unpleasant task is not something a healthy man would want to face twice in a single lifetime.

No such luck for Nathan, however. He picks up the palace scuttlebutt as rapidly as the next person: the hanky-panky between David and Bathsheba has involved not only *(a)* adultery but also *(b)* deception and *(c)* murder. And by any standard of moral conduct, David is guilty on all three counts, only he doesn't know it, and somebody has to point it out, which is a clear entrance cue for a prophet, although Nathan would probably have preferred to put in for a leave of absence at this point, with or without pay. Calling a king to account, challenging the highest earthly authority one knows, is no small matter. The one who does so had better be committed to something or someone more ultimate than the king, be sure of his facts, and possess a clear, well-modulated voice. Nathan apparently scores well in all three departments . . . plus the fact that he too, like a military commander, is "under orders." That's what being a prophet is all about. The biblical text connecting chapters 11 and 12 makes this very clear: "But the thing that David had done displeased the LORD. And the LORD sent Nathan to David" (2 Samuel

11:27–12:1). Showdown time has come. And Nathan has to put all his security up for grabs.

3. *The Ewe Lamb Story* is the way Nathan traps the king into an admission of guilt. We need not linger over it save to notice how devastatingly David indicts himself out of his own mouth and how Nathan responds.

Nathan's device is simplicity itself. He tells the king a story: Once upon a time there was a rich man with plenty of sheep. But when a guest came for dinner, the rich man stole the one ewe lamb that a poor man owned and loved, slaughtered it, and fed it to the guest. End of story.

David is indignant. What injustice! What a travesty of human relations! Such a one should die! Let him at least repay the poor man fourfold for his gross theft of that which belonged to another!

Nathan springs the trap. Four words are enough: "You are the man" (2 Sam. 12:7).

And that is really as far as we need to carry the tale, although Nathan goes on to make sure the point isn't lost, and certain analogies between the rich man, the poor man, and the ewe lamb and David, Uriah, and Bathsheba emerge rather clearly.

In any case, David sees the point and repents, saying, "I have sinned against the LORD" (2 Sam. 12:13). A heavy price is paid: the son born of the illicit relationship dies. But out of the union of David and Bathsheba comes another son, Solomon, who goes on to ambiguous heights of greatness as the successor to his father's dynasty.

And Nathan survives. It is not always the case that those who stand up against iniquity in high places survive, and those who plan to stand up against iniquity in high places had better not weave survival too centrally into their plans. That is why it is best to end the story with Nathan's ringing and unambiguous challenge to David, "You are the man"—you are the one who has sinned, and you must be called to account, whatever the price.

OTHER BIBLICAL PASSAGES

The "no" to authority, the unwillingness to bend the knee uncritically to those with power, is a recurring biblical story, a fleshing-out of the meaning of the First Commandment, "You shall have no other gods before me" (Ex. 20:3). The Nathan syndrome is everywhere.

We have already encountered Moses standing up to Pharaoh, and while Moses (like Nathan) had a more ultimate commitment to Yahweh than to the king, and (like Nathan) was sure of his facts, he did not (unlike Nathan) have a clear, well-modulated voice. As we have already noticed, he stuttered badly and tried, unsuccessfully, to escape being Yahweh's mouthpiece, offering his speech impediment as a pretext for disengagement. This is a consoling tale for those lacking oratorical skills: they can still be used.

Almost every biblical prophet, well-modulated voice or not, is called upon to say no to the establishment, usually personified in the king. We will mention this again in Chapter 4, when we see how Jeremiah gives King Jehoiakim an even harder time than Nathan gave King David. Jesus, we have already noted, is crucified as a threat to political stability.

Jesus' followers made their own contribution to the cause. While it took Nathan four words to level the indictment, it took the early Christians only two. The Greek words initially sound innocuous: *"Kyrios Christos,"* meaning "Christ is Lord." It was a way in which Christians could identify their *kyrios,* their "lord," which means their highest object of allegiance, than whom there is nothing more ultimate.

All of which could hardly have disturbed the Roman authorities less, save for one inconvenient fact: they demanded an annually renewed oath of allegiance from all citizens that went (with the same economy of language), *"Kyrios Caesar,"* meaning "Caesar (the state) is Lord." It was a way in which Roman citizens could identify their *kyrios,* their "lord"—their highest object of allegiance, than whom there is nothing more ultimate. It was a case of the immovable object confronting the irresistible force. For it was soon obvious to the Roman authorities that no one could make *both* statements simultaneously without lying, or sequentially without a massive conversion experience in between. So when Christians said *"Kyrios Christos"* they were doing two things: (1) they were saying, "Christ is the ultimate power in our lives, before whom everything else is subordinate," and (2) they were also saying, "Caesar, the state, is *not* the ultimate power in our lives but is in fact subordinate."

That was very much in line with the biblical witness and very much out of line with the expectations of the Roman authorities, which could be reduced to the formula "The Empire—Love It or Leave It," and in relation to which the Roman authorities provided very efficient exit gates from a waiting room in the Colosseum to an arena filled with hungry lions, in case anybody decided to leave.

The hardier Christians, however, stayed by their creed, which did not change. And they learned that to say yes to God provides power to say no to those who aspire to be God and are not God. But that is a story that takes nineteen centuries to tell.

ITEMS FOR REFLECTION AND DISCUSSION

If we assume that Nathan was not a fool, and that his action was exemplary, we are left with the problem of how to replicate that action in our own life and times.

1. Reinhold Niebuhr once said, apropos of the need to turn our critical faculties upon ourselves as well as upon those with whom we disagree, "We must fight their falsehood with our truth, but we must also fight the falsehood in our truth." How would this relate to U.S. attempts to impose "our way of life" on Central American nations?

2. Who are those who stand today as contemporary counter-

parts of Nathan? What are some of the situations today in which new Nathans are needed?

3. Christians in Germany faced the same problem in the 1930s that Christians in the Roman Empire faced in the A.D. 30s. Hitler had come to power and was demanding absolute allegiance. Criticism, public or private, could not be brooked. He was *der Führer,* "the leader," who was beyond possibility of criticism—a modern *kyrios.* Most of the German culture capitulated—the universities, the business world, the church. But a few within the church did not. Martin Niemöller, a pastor in Berlin, joined the issue decisively with a book of sermons entitled *Christus ist mein Führer* (Christ Is My Leader), self-consciously adopting the Nazi vocabulary for the purpose of turning it to ends for which it was never intended. Since Christ is my "leader"—Niemöller was saying—Hitler is *not* my "leader." There cannot be two highest allegiances but only one. And to say yes to Christ is to say no to Hitler.

Martin Niemöller spent seven years in a concentration camp, but his witness was widened in the Confessing Church, which he helped to found and which issued the Barmen Declaration in 1934, declaring that "Jesus Christ . . . is the one Word of God whom we have to hear, trust, and obey in life and in death." Without ever mentioning Hitler by name, the writers of the Declaration made clear that their affirmation of Christ's claim was their repudiation of Hitler's claims. The Nazis got the message. A lot of members of the Confessing Church ended up in the camps too.

There are people in the United States who feel that it is time for a Confessing Church or a Barmen Declaration of our own. Does this seem farfetched and paranoid, or are there indications here at home that we need to find ways to say no to certain claims and policies of our government?

4. The David-Nathan episode illustrates *the power of a story.* We usually think of stories as pleasant diversions from the sterner aspects of life, something we read to children or indulge

in when we've gotten caught up on more "important" things. Many people confess to a lingering sense of guilt when they turn to fiction instead of "serious" reading.

And yet, as Nathan's account of the ewe lamb shows, stories have a way of sneaking past our defenses and forcing us to look at things in a new way. One can imagine how tense and defensive David must have been when Nathan requested an audience, sure that Nathan had picked up the palace gossip and was about to nail him to the wall. One can also imagine the infinite relief with which David must have heard Nathan begin with the lulling phrase, "Once upon a time . . ." Entertainment, not judgment, was to be the order of the day.

As we have seen, however, the relief was short-lived, and the audience granted to Nathan did not turn out to be lulling time after all. For the story about an innocent lamb was not really a story about an innocent lamb but a story about a guilty king, told in such a way that David was drawn too deeply into it to extricate himself when he finally discovered that the story was his own.

Nathan's comment "You are the man!" broke down whatever remaining walls David might have wanted to retain between the two stories. And by being brought into the ewe lamb story, David suddenly saw, in what must have been a sickening moment of insight, that he had been reading incorrectly not only the ewe lamb story but his own story as well, which up to that point had gone, "Kings are entitled to whatever they want and are entitled to get it by whatever means they choose." Now, however, in the light of the ewe lamb story, David saw that a corrected version of his own story must become normative for him: "Kings are as accountable as anybody else and must pay the consequences when they do wrong."

5. A one-sided (?) thought starter:

David Mammon, chief executive officer of Guaranty Rural Amalgamated Businesses (GRAB), was looking over the export-import figures of a small rural country in Central America.

There were photographs with the report, showing a country dotted with small farms. "We could do a much better job with those natural resources," he reflected, "than the natives. All they do is grow enough for themselves plus a little bit to export. We could turn the whole countryside into a vast coffee plantation and make tremendous profits by exporting the coffee overseas."

And, such being the resources of GRAB, it came to be as he had wished. Within a decade the dictator running the country had expropriated all the small farms and leased the land to GRAB. Farmers who refused to vacate found their houses and crops mysteriously burned. The whole countryside became a coffee plantation. Some of the farmers were reemployed by GRAB, but their wages were too low to buy enough food for their families, which they had to do, since nothing but coffee was now grown on the land they had formerly cultivated, and coffee, they discovered, did not provide a sufficiently well-rounded diet for their children. The only place they could purchase food was in stores owned by GRAB.

When the few who had been reemployed began to organize to secure better wages and better working conditions, they were told that if they didn't like their wages they could quit, since there were plenty of unemployed people who would be glad to have their jobs. Those who had been directly involved in the organizing were fired outright, and there was an additional message in the form of bullets fired through the walls of their houses after dark by persons unknown and never apprehended. The dictator and the GRAB officials publicly deplored the action.

One Sunday after these things had come to pass, David Mammon went to church. He was an active church member who sang in the choir and advised the parish council about maximum-growth investments. For the Old Testament lesson, the minister read a quaint tale about a rich man who had great herds of sheep and a poor man who had only one tiny lamb that was the joy of his life. But when a traveler visited the rich man, the rich man stole the ewe lamb from the poor man and ordered his servants to cook it for the evening banquet.

David Mammon was incensed. What a way to treat the poor man, taking his one possession and destroying it, when the rich man already had sheep and to spare! In the coffee hour afterward, Mammon said heatedly, "He should have had to pay the poor man back at least four times as much as he stole."

But there was no Nathan to point to David and say, "You are the man."

4. JEREMIAH AND JEHOIAKIM: TO KNOW GOD IS TO DO JUSTICE
(Changing Priorities)

Jeremiah 22:13–17

What does it mean to "know God"? Who are the ones who know God?

The questions seem simple and answers come immediately to mind. Those who know God are the ones who have had some experience of God about which they are able to tell us—sometimes a little too easily and glibly to be fully convincing, but sometimes in halting and fumbling ways that are themselves authentic pointers to the magnitude and awesomeness of the encounter they are trying to describe. Such people will tell us that they have found God in the face of another person, or in a sunset, or in a compulsion to obey a moral demand, or in a sense of the immensity of space and their own smallness, or by reading the Bible, or through meditating on the life of Jesus. The ones we call the "saints" are often those from whom we get our clearest picture of what it must be like to know God; their lives of prayer and meditation and good works have a transparent goodness that makes their appeal to the name and will of God convincing and compelling.

In contrast to such people, we know other people who make no such claims whatever. They do not go to church or read the Bible or pray, and the name of God, if ever found upon their lips, may be uttered more in exasperation than exaltation. For some of them, God is simply not an issue, and they live good, decent lives apparently unruffled by concern about God's reality or nonreality. A few, at least, are militant in their denial of God and scornful of those who still affirm God; atheism has become their "religion" and they wonder how others can be so benighted as to give allegiance to an outworn myth. For still others, God is something or someone they have consciously discarded, often wistfully and even sadly. They would like to believe. But if God was ever real for them, God no longer is. They may live exemplary lives, exhibit concern for the neighbor, even make sacrifices for the cause of the poor and the destitute. But they no longer claim to "know God."

The above description is fairly commonplace and may even have drawn nods of assent. But we will be doing serious violation to the Bible's understanding of what it means to "know God" if we leave it at that. There is a short—and startling—episode in the book of Jeremiah that poses the question of "knowing God" in quite another way.

THE BIBLICAL TEXT: JEREMIAH 22:13–17

> [13]"Woe to him who builds his house by unrighteousness,
>   and his upper rooms by injustice;
>   who makes his neighbor serve him for nothing,
>   and does not give him his wages;
> [14]who says, 'I will build myself a great house
>   with spacious upper rooms,'
>   and cuts out windows for it,
>   paneling it with cedar,
>   and painting it with vermilion.
> [15]Do you think you are a king
>   because you compete in cedar?
>   Did not your father eat and drink
>   and do justice and righteousness?
>   Then it was well with him.
> [16]He judged the cause of the poor and needy;
>   then it was well.
>   Is not this to know me?
> >   says the LORD.

¹⁷But you have eyes and heart
only for your dishonest gain,
for shedding innocent blood,
and for practicing oppression and violence."

Throughout the passage, as we can see, Jeremiah is inveighing against the king—a favorite indoor sport of prophets, as we have already discovered from our encounter with Nathan. Jehoiakim (who reigned 609–598 B.C.) was the son of King Josiah, who had instituted important reforms and whose death had been widely mourned. Perhaps that was part of Jehoiakim's problem. But Egypt was another part of his problem, and in the early part of his reign he was so much under the thumb of the mighty Egyptian empire to the south that he even had to extract tribute money for Egypt from the taxes levied against his own people.

What has Jehoiakim been up to that incenses Jeremiah so much that his very first word is "Woe . . ."? The answer seems pretty clear: the king is building a new palace, and it is not just an ordinary run-of-the-mill ranch-style palace; this one will have two stories and will be "spacious" beyond all normal needs, with picture windows, radiant heating, and a fourteen-stall garage. Instead of ordinary pine paneling, available at the local lumber mill, it will be finished off in cedar, a rare and expensive wood that has to be imported and milled by hand. Nor will the palace be painted in soft colors to harmonize with the landscape; instead, it will be painted vermilion—bright, garish, attention-getting.

But the king's excessiveness is not the only reason for Jeremiah's bombastic attack. The real problem is not only that the end product is *unnecessary* but that the means of building it are *unjust*. The palace is being built by "unrighteousness," the upper rooms by "injustice." Jehoiakim is not only using slave labor but refusing to pay the workers. The king, at the top of the heap, is accumulating even greater goods for himself by exploiting those at the bottom. It is a rerun of the Egyptian

scene we looked at earlier, with a slightly different cast of characters, which is to say that it is still the classic oppressor-
oppressed model, in which the rich get richer while the poor get
poorer.

At the end of the passage Jeremiah says as much, indicting
Jehoiakim "for practicing oppression and violence" (Jer. 22:17).
The Hebrew word for "violence" used here, *ratsats,* is especially
graphic; it means "to mash, grind, or crush," which is precisely
what Jehoiakim's labor policy is accomplishing.

Jeremiah's opening barrage is a simple, direct account of what
is going on, delivered, we may be sure, in less than dulcet tones:
"Woe to him [guess who, O king?] who makes his neighbor [ha!]
serve him for nothing [for nothing! can you imagine it? for
nothing?]" (Jer. 22:13–14).

Barely warmed up, Jeremiah asks a scathing question: "Do
you think you are a king because you compete in cedar?" (Jer.
22:15). Do you think the Egyptian envoy will be impressed that
you are gilding the lily by using *cedar* to panel your palace, and
that this will somehow earn you points in Memphis or Thebes,
while people here are starving in the process?

In full throttle now, Jeremiah does a clever, cruel thing: he
compares the king to his father, which is a type of putdown
grown men don't need. "Did not your father eat and drink
and do justice and righteousness? Then it was well with him"
(Jer. 22:15). The question probes in several directions. We
know that the father *did* "eat and drink"—that is to say, he
wasn't an ascetic, mortifying the body, and can't be written off
as some impractical visionary who need not be taken seriously.
But, as some commentators suggest, the reference to eating
and drinking may also refer to the "covenant meal" with Yahweh: "justice and righteousness," for which Josiah is immediately commended, were constituent parts of the covenant.
Martin Buber, an eminent Jewish scholar, comments: "[Jo-
siah] takes part in the holy covenant meal, enters the covenant
with YHVH, and henceforth fulfils it by himself practicing

justice and righteousness, and as regards men by vindicating the cause of the poor and needy" (*The Prophetic Faith,* pp. 162–163; Macmillan Co., 1949). In either case, "eating and drinking" are not antithetical to, but complementary to, doing "justice and righteousness." If that is what characterized Josiah, it is exactly the reverse of what characterizes Jehoiakim, who is building the palace by "*in*justice and *un*righteousness." So, if "it was well" with Josiah, it is far from well with Jehoiakim.

To dispel any lingering doubts, Jeremiah makes the point again with a simple declarative statement: "[Josiah] judged the cause of the poor and needy; then it was well" (Jer. 22:16). Doing "justice and righteousness" is the same thing as taking up "the cause of the poor and needy."

On Jeremiah's reckoning, then, Jehoiakim emerges quite a few cuts below the old man, and that assessment alone must have made Jehoiakim want to consign Jeremiah to the deepest well around, one with smooth siding and no footholds.

But Jeremiah still isn't through; the *coup de grâce* is still to come. Jeremiah draws the threads of the argument together in the form of a rhetorical question: "All this doing of justice and righteousness, all this vindicating of the poor and needy—isn't this what it means to know me? the Lord says."

Says, not asks. . . . The form of the construction allows only for an affirmative answer. Conclusion: to know God *is* to do justice and righteousness, to vindicate the poor and the needy. And so Jeremiah draws the descriptive conclusion that Jehoiakim is doing just the opposite; he is shedding innocent blood and "practicing oppression and violence" (Jer. 22:17). Second conclusion: therefore he doesn't know God. Third conclusion (later in the chapter): he won't get away with it, and his doing of injustice will bring about his downfall.

The conclusions are either devastating or promising (particularly the one that goes "to know God is to do justice"), depending on whether *you* are "doing justice" or not. All over Latin

America, poor and oppressed peoples have adopted that phrase and use it as a measuring rod of political discrimination and an ongoing sign of hope: *Conocer a Dios es obrar la justicia,* to know God is to do justice.

To know God is not (necessarily) to go to mass every Sunday or say the Rosary every day. It is not (necessarily) to know the Apostles' Creed or be able to make a perfect act of contrition. One can do all those things and still not know God. Rather, to know God is "to achieve justice for the poor." As José Miranda, a Mexican biblical scholar puts it, "Jahweh is known only in the human act of achieving justice and compassion for the neighbor" (Miranda, *Marx and the Bible,* p. 49). So to know God might mean working in a political party to overthrow a modern counterpart of Jehoiakim. It might mean saying no to economic or religious structures that provide privileges for the rich at the expense of the poor. It might mean joining a labor union in areas where labor unions are outlawed, since in no other way would the poor be able to gain enough power to demand just working conditions and just wages.

So God will not be found, Miranda goes on (referring to various abstractions Christians use) "among the 'entities,' nor the 'existings,' nor in 'univocal being,' nor in 'analogous being,' but rather in the implacable moral imperative of justice" (p. 49, slightly adapted).

Even more graphically, the Latin American novelist José María Arguedas, in *Todas las sangres,* has a sacristan respond to a priest who has said glibly, "God is everywhere."

> Was God in the heart of those who broke the body of the innocent teacher Bellido? Is God in the bodies of engineers who are killing "La Esmeralda"? In the official who took the corn fields away from their owners? (Cited in Gutiérrez, *A Theology of Liberation,* p. 195)

Once again, the question is rhetorical. The only possible answer is "Of course not!" God will *not* be found in the midst of such injustice. Where, then, will God be found and known? In the doing of justice, in making one's own the cause of the poor, in breaking with systems of oppression, in joining the struggle with the victims.

OTHER BIBLICAL PASSAGES

This notion, so strange to us—that "knowing God" is a matter of deed rather than word, that one could affirm God without saying God's name or deny God while God's name was on one's lips—is not at all strange to the Bible. The Jeremiah passage is not the exception but the rule.

In Isaiah 10:5–11 we have the astonishing declaration that the leader of the Assyrian nation, Israel's enemy, is actually God's "rod" and "staff" and will be used by God for the fulfillment of God's purposes, since God's own people, Israel, have turned away from God and can, for the moment at least, be described only as "a godless nation" (Isa. 10:6). Here is an absolute reversal of expectation and definition: the one we would call the "godless nation," Assyria, is God's instrument, while the one we would call God's instrument, Israel, is the "godless nation."

To be sure, the Assyrian king does not know he is God's instrument: "he does not so intend, and his mind does not so think" (Isa. 10:7), and in the end he too will be brought low. But we must not use the ultimate downfall of the king of Assyria as a means of glossing over the central assertion of the passage: namely, that if one does not do justice (i.e., God's will), one does not know God and can only be appropriately described as "godless."

Jesus makes the point even more simply and directly in a statement that is a close analogue to the Jeremiah passage: "Not every one who says to me, 'Lord, Lord,' shall enter the kingdom of heaven, but [the one] who does the will of my Father who is in heaven" (Matt. 7:21). No elaboration necessary.

The same theme is present in the Johannine literature. The

venerable author, writing to an early Christian community, is talking about love, but as we discover repeatedly, the line between love and justice is exceedingly thin and finally nonexistent. There is no love without justice, no justice without love. So we can claim this passage as another New Testament version of the Jeremiah theme: "Beloved, let us love one another; for love is of God, and anyone who loves is born of God and knows God. One who does not love does not know God; for God is love" (1 John 4:7–8, adapted). The one who loves knows God; the one who does not love does not know God. A claim could hardly be more unequivocal.

It is clear through the letter as a whole that God is "known" only through the neighbor: "Those who do not love the brothers or sisters whom they can see, cannot love God whom they have never seen" (1 John 4:20, adapted). As Miranda says, commenting on the letter as a whole, the revelation of God "is possible only *through the neighbor who must be loved.* . . . God is not God when we try to approach [God] while avoiding our neighbor" (pp. 64, 65).

ITEMS FOR REFLECTION AND DISCUSSION

Where does all this leave us? The following proposals are designed to help readers continue to confront the text:

1. Just what is "justice"? Notice how the passage itself seems to answer the question not by offering abstract definitions but by pointing to examples of *doing* justice. How do they translate to our situation? Discuss Aristotle's definition of justice as "rendering to each person his or her due," and a recent refinement, "rendering to each child his or her due." What is "due" anyone? Who decides? Who renders what is "due"? Individuals? Charitable organizations? The government? Must all people have the same rights guaranteed to them?

2. If "to know God is to do justice," does it follow that "to do injustice is not to know God"?

3. Do you agree or disagree that the account of conditions in
the Jeremiah passage is a microcosm of our own world as well?
Is it true today, as in the time of Jeremiah, that the rich get
richer while the poor get poorer? (Information: At the end of
the United Nations "Decade of Development" [1960–1970],
when a special effort was made to *close the gap* between the rich
and the poor, the relative gap between them had increased
rather than decreased. During this period, the United States of
America, with about 6 percent of the world's population, was
consuming about 40 percent of the world's resources.)

4. In order to get the full flavor of the biblical passage, try
role-playing the various characters in the story, using the following examples only to get started:

JEHOIAKIM: Who is this klutz Jeremiah to tell me off?
What does he know about the problems of power? As for
paying the palace workers, did Jeremiah ever have to meet
a payroll? There are always going to be poor people, and
they ought to be grateful for food and shelter without
worrying about wages. If we started paying them what he
would call a "living wage," the economy would suffer,
people would stop investing, and the workers would want
coffee breaks, a union, and an insurance scheme to cover
on-the-job disabilities. Somebody ought to give Jeremiah a
crash course on cost-benefit analysis, or at least persuade
him that religion and economics don't mix. And as for
dragging in my father—

JEREMIAH: Look, I didn't want to be a prophet. It's no fun
taking the side of the underdog and getting thrown down
the village well, let alone being the laughingstock of the
whole palace crowd. But if that's the way it has to be, I've
got to report the Lord's will as accurately as I can. And
that's going to be continual bad news for Jehoiakim, since
justice is the name of the game. If people want to "know
God," it won't be enough to offer burnt offerings, or tithe,
or memorize the Westminster Catechism, or go to prayer

breakfasts in the nation's capital. Those things mean *nothing* in comparison to doing justice, and less than nothing when they become cover-ups for injustice.

THE WORKERS: "Justice," the man says. Well, we may not know much about justice, but we know a lot about injustice. Look at us! They work us to the bone, set up quotas for how much we have to get done each day, and then raise the quotas about every third week. When we try to organize, they beat up the union organizers. When we complain, they say, "You're lucky to have any job at all. A *lot* of people would work for just room and board and be grateful. You'd better begin to know when you're well off."

GOD [this may seem presumptuous, but we have Jeremiah and the rest of Scripture to give us some clues]: Did I, after all, give you humans too much freedom? You use it so badly, making things worse for each other all the time. Why can't you get the word, *my* word? I'm not interested in your sacrifices and your "religious" activities; all they seem to do is create new barriers between you. If you want to "know" me, start caring for each other, and let justice roll down like waters and righteousness like a mighty stream. I see you coming into the sanctuary with a gift for me while you still have a grudge against your brother or sister. And I want to shout to you, "Please! Leave the gift by the altar and go make it up with your brother or sister and *then* come and offer me the gift." Under those circumstances I'll be pleased to have it. You seem to want to offer me praise while your whole society is grinding people down and destroying them. Please, offer me praise by exalting the victims of your society rather than exploiting them; enlist their help in creating a society where there are decent jobs, safe working conditions, and a sense of dignity for all people, just the opposite of what Jehoiakim is offering. No more exploitation, if you really want to "know" me.

5. How do third world Christians react after hearing a passage like Jeremiah 22? Listen to Elsa Tamez, a biblical scholar from Costa Rica:

> Today we ask: How can those in command of oppressive regimes participate in the Eucharist, since all their actions are a denial of the gospel of life? How can the name of Christian be claimed by the stockholders in the great corporations, or by those who monopolize the means of production and exploit workers in such deadly ways; or by those who talk of human rights but at the same time approve shipments of military aid to dictatorial regimes so that the latter may open the door to the multinational corporations? (*Bible of the Oppressed,* pp. 79–80)

What is your reaction to her reaction?

5. MARY'S SONG:
WHOM DO WE HEAR?
(Changing Perspectives)

Luke 1:46–55

We turn on the classical radio station in the midst of ethereal music that permeates our tough exteriors and touches an inner core of response. We can't understand the words—they're in Latin, as it turns out—but there is no doubt that the melodies, instruments, and voices are communicating spirituality at its best.

The music stops and the announcer tells us that we have been listening to the Magnificat by di Lassus (who wrote the one I heard most recently) or Frescobaldi or Vivaldi or Palestrina or Mozart or Berlioz or Pinkham or, if we're really lucky, Johann Sebastian Bach. There is no single passage of Scripture more frequently set to music.

We're less familiar with the words that have received so much musical attention. We hear the passage once a year in church during Advent, when it is combined with the story of the Annunciation. The picture we register is that of a dutiful peasant girl, overwhelmed by the presence of an angel, who is meekly subservient to God: "Behold the handmaid of the Lord; be it unto me according to thy word" (Luke 1:38), she responds in good Elizabethan English. We find it charming.

But there is nothing charming in the song that the alleged dutiful peasant girl sings a bit later, a musical prayer we call "The Magnificat," because in Jerome's Latin version the first words are *Magnificat anima mea Dominum,* "My soul magnifies the Lord."

Studying the passage will furnish a telling example of how selectively we listen and how efficiently we filter out what we don't want to hear.

THE BIBLICAL TEXT: LUKE 1:46–55

"My soul magnifies the Lord,
[47]and my spirit rejoices in God my Savior,
[48]who has regarded the low estate of God's handmaiden.
For behold, henceforth all generations will call me blessed;
[49]for God who is mighty has done great things for me,
and holy is God's name.

[50]And God's mercy is on those who fear God
from generation to generation.
[51]God has shown strength with God's arm,
has scattered the proud in the imagination of their hearts,
[52]put down the mighty from their thrones,
and exalted those of low degree;
[53]has filled the hungry with good things,
and the rich has sent empty away.
[54]God has helped God's servant Israel,
remembering to show mercy,
[55]as God spoke to our fathers,
to Abraham and to his posterity forever."

(Adapted)

The first two chapters of Luke give us our fullest account of Jesus' birth and childhood. They are interpretive rather than reportorial, and we read them to the backdrop of Christmas pageants—children wearing bathrobes as they move from being shepherds standing on a hillside to shepherds kneeling in a barn before a crèche, in which a 75-watt bulb communicates the presence of divinity. There's a gentle harmony to it all.

Into the harmony, however, comes a discordant note. We call
it Mary's song, though there can be legitimate questions about
whether she sang it in anything like its present form. Some
manuscripts, in fact, attribute it to her cousin Elizabeth, and all
manuscripts display close parallels to an earlier song by another
mother, Hannah, to which we will shortly turn. One modern
commentary finds so much editing within the present text as to
conclude that it is "a ponderous piece of poetry with little
originality or imagination," though conceding that "it expresses
deep emotion and strong conviction." The second comment is
more accurate than the first.

The song is important to us for at least two reasons: (1) it
reiterates themes so much a part of Jewish tradition that Luke
could not do justice to the birth of a Jewish child without
including them; and (2) the importance of those themes is em-
phasized by putting them on the lips of Jesus' mother, who plays
a central role in the story.

Mary is a lower-class working girl in Nazareth, engaged to a
local carpenter. She has a troubling vision in the midst of the
morning dusting: an angel appears, understandably frightening
her out of her wits, since angels, in the biblical tradition, are
messengers of God, and what is a messenger of God doing with
the likes of her? Even more troubling than the angel's presence,
however, is the angel's message: Mary is going to have a baby.
And since Mary, on her own testimony, has not yet slept with
Joseph, or anyone else for that matter, she is more than a little
mystified as to how this could happen. There is also the considerable dilemma of what she is going to tell her fiancé. For if
Mary is mystified, one can imagine Joseph's perplexity—a perplexity that was the topic of ribald comedy-relief interludes in
the medieval mystery plays.

Be that as it may, Mary, who has little choice, accepts the
word of the angel that in her womb the Messianic hope will
come to fruition in just nine months' time. *Her* son, son of a
nobody, will be the "Son of the Most High," of whose "kingdom

there will be no end" (Luke 1:32–33). Wow!

Mary, still in a dazzled state, goes up into the hill country to visit her elderly cousin Elizabeth, herself six months into a totally unexpected pregnancy. It is during the visit that Mary sings her song. It is in two parts: her exultation at what God is doing for *her* (Luke 1:47–49), and her exultation at what God is doing for *Israel* (Luke 1:50–55). The two parts of the song, which we have separated by a space in our printed text, have a common theme: that which was lowly is being lifted up, that which was high is being cast down. And it is all God's doing.

It is also all very political. We have managed to hide this fact from ourselves, but it is a fact that has led our sisters and brothers in the third world to give the song a central place in their lives. And so the question to us goes: Can we move beyond the comfortably demure Mary of our tradition to the uncomfortably militant Mary of their tradition?

It strikes us as strange, to start with, that a political perspective would be found in a prayer. Politics and *singing* we can understand—after all, the great political themes of the 1960s were enunciated by the folksingers, and in every modern revolution it seems to be the musicians who articulate the hopes of the masses. The dictators know this. When General Pinochet and his U.S.-backed junta seized power in the coup in Chile that we explored in Chapter 2, they chopped off the hands of Victor Jara, whose guitar playing had been a catalyst for the hopes of the poor and oppressed.

Politics and song, yes. But politics *and prayer?* That goes against our desire to keep life compartmentalized: "religious" activities here, "political" activities there. But Mary's song cuts through all that tidiness, just as the son she is carrying will do later on, challenging the Herods and the Caesars, doing "secular" things on the Sabbath like picking corn and healing the sick, and getting arrested and killed as a threat to the political order. To start with God (as Mary's song does) and end with God (as her song also does) means lots and lots of politics in between (as the intervening verses demonstrate).

Mary, then, begins with praise: her soul magnifies the Lord and her spirit rejoices in God her Savior. Why? Because in her, God has turned things upside down. Another kind of God, if about to send a Son into the world, would surely have chosen a mother from royalty, or at least from the ranks of the upper class. But not *this* God to whom Mary is singing; no, this God has stooped to regard "the low estate of God's handmaiden" (Luke 1:48; some translations have "slave" instead of "hand-maiden," which makes the point even more vividly). *This* God pays special attention to the poor, the oppressed, the enslaved. You are looking for a Savior? Don't look to the royal courts, look among the slaves. Don't look to the capital city, Jerusalem, look to the boondocks, Nazareth. "Can anything good come out of Nazareth?" (John 1:46), they later taunted, and the very tone of the question refuted in advance the claims of anyone who came from there.

But God is not beholden to human estimates of worth. It is a peasant girl, one of no account, whom God raises up, so that henceforth all generations will call her blessed (cf. Luke 1:48). Mary can hardly believe it: "God who is mighty has done great things for me" (Luke 1:49)—for *me,* Mary What's-her-name from the wrong side of the tracks, the one with no education, no coming-out party, no executive position in the corporate structure of a multinational corporation, the one who is the object of a lot of sly talk and gossip ("Impregnated by the Holy Ghost indeed! A likely story . . ."). If this is the way God operates, all bets are off. Our assessments of who is important must be put on hold.

We can handle that on an *individual* level. After all, people with names like Yastrzemski occasionally make it big in the Boston of the Cabots and the Lodges, and people with skin color departing from the norm, like Martin Luther King, Jr., have national holidays declared in their honor.

But what if that were meant to describe the *social* patterns as well, so that lowly *groups* were raised up, and those in the groups now on top were cast down? It is with just such disturbing notions that Mary's song continues, as she moves from singing about herself to singing about *all* who worship God "from generation to generation" (Luke 1:50). What will it be like when the reversals come at the hand of a God whose arm "has shown strength" (Luke 1:51)?

First of all, Mary clears the decks:

"God has scattered the proud in the imagination of their hearts." Those who think they have it put together, those surest of themselves, those most successful in establishing confident self-images, will be "scattered," beyond any hope of putting it all together again.

Then Mary (or her librettist) offers two vivid contrasts between the lowly raised up and the high brought low. The first is political, the second economic, although each category contains the other.

The political (and economic) contrast:

"God has put down the mighty from their thrones . . ." Israel had seen a succession of empires rise and fall: Assyria, Babylonia, Egypt, Greece. We have seen the same: the nineteenth-century British Empire, the twentieth-century Third Reich. Today, Americans expect Russia to topple while Russians anticipate America's demise. Political power is never secure, always vulnerable. But people never expect *their own* nation to be "put down," so that is the word we need to hear: perhaps America is toppling.

"The mighty" are not only political nations and empires but economic manipulators of other people's destinies, those who decide which plant will close and which stay open; or decide that Nicaragua must fall regardless of what the people of Nicaragua want; or decree that their corporation will destroy an independent company through a price war, since they can sustain a loss until the smaller competitor gives up.

". . . and exalted those of low degree." Mary is saying that

"those of low degree," meaning those without power—the oppressed, the no-account, the poor—are the ones God will lift up. Israel has outlasted Assyria, Babylon, Egypt, and Greece; the workers will outlast the board executives who close the plants; the peasants of Nicaragua will be vindicated against the "giant from the north"; the small company will come back when the multinational has faded from the scene.

The economic (and political) contrast:

"God has filled the hungry with good things . . ." Imagine the hope such a claim would engender in the two thirds of the human family who go to bed hungry every night. The political implications of the hope are obvious to them. Waiting around for the rich to feed the poor isn't the way to go, so the poor will have to take matters into their own hands. Yes, God will fill their mouths, but God expects them to help. At the time of the exodus, God could show the people the way to the Promised Land, but the people themselves had to undertake the journey. Similarly, in the matter of hunger, with which Mary is dealing here, the people will have to challenge political and economic systems that help the rich get richer while the poor get poorer, and insist on land redistribution so that all can own some rather than a few owning all. The planet can support its population, but only with radically different methods of sharing land, distribution, and profits.

". . . and the rich has sent empty away." If God does "fill the hungry with good things," that means less for the nonhungry, for whom Mary uses the word "rich." They have a bleak future in her scenario. Perhaps those who are rich, if ready to be nonrich, can survive. That will be a choice for them to ponder while there is still time.

There is a final claim, so strange that we seldom notice it:

"God has helped God's servant Israel . . ." God helping a servant? Surely it is the other way around: servants help masters. But Mary informs us that "the other way around" has become the wrong way around. The One who needs nothing helps those

who need everything. It's all in reverse. And if servants are around to be "helped," then they are no longer servants but something else. Friends, companions, equals? . . .

Mary sings not only of servants in general but of "servant Israel" in particular. And if there is any claim that turns things upside down, it is the claim that Israel stands in a special relationship to God. If Mary as an individual is a nobody, Israel as a nation is even more of a nobody. One could have looked in many directions in the ancient world for a nation to represent God: Egypt with its culture, Rome with its cosmopolitan character, Greece with its philosophers and tragedians, Babylon with its mighty warriors, Assyria . . . but Israel? To have selected Israel as a means for saving the world in those days is as though today we pinned our hopes for world peace on Andorra.

To our third world friends, the Messianic event (which is what the song points toward) will not just be a spiritual realignment of eternal values but a starkly political and social reversal. As Elsa Tamez puts it, Mary's song does not speak "of individuals undergoing moral change but of *the restructuring of the order* in which there are rich and poor, mighty and lowly" (*Bible of the Oppressed,* p. 68, italics added). And Gustavo Gutiérrez, after noting how the first part of the song emphasizes joy in being loved by God (cf. Luke 1:47–49), reminds us that thanksgiving and joy "are closely linked to the action of God who liberates the oppressed and humbles the powerful." His hopeful conclusion is that "the future of history belongs to the poor and exploited. True liberation will be the work of the oppressed themselves; in them, the Lord saves history" (*A Theology of Liberation,* p. 208). Mary's song is a call to revolutionary action.

ANOTHER BIBLICAL PASSAGE

There are foreshadowings of Mary's song in a passage on which Luke has clearly drawn, the song of Hannah in 1 Sam. 2:1–10. It sounds more like a song of thanksgiving for the nation

than for an individual, and it may be a later insertion in the
narrative. But there are many shared themes in the two poems.
The circumstances of the two women are somewhat different.
Mary, as we have seen, is unmarried and pregnant; her song
comes before the baby is born. Hannah has been married many
years and never been pregnant. She is constantly twitted by her
husband's other wife, who seems to have been as fertile as
Hannah was barren. Finally, however, after a session of ago-
nized praying in the temple at Shiloh (she is so agitated that the
high priest thinks she is drunk), Hannah's wish is granted and
she l er gives birth to a son, whom she consecrates to God. Her
song comes after the baby is born.

She begins with words that find a clear echo in Mary's song:

> My heart exults in the LORD,
>   my strength is exalted in the LORD. (V. 1)

She makes obeisance to the tremendous power of God (vs. 2, 7)
and then sings of how such a God exercises power:

> The bows of the mighty are broken,
>   but the feeble gird on strength.
> Those who were full have hired themselves out for bread,
>   but those who were hungry have ceased to hunger. (Vs. 4–5)

> The LORD raises up the poor from the dust;
>   and lifts the needy from the ash heap,
> to make them sit with princes
>   and inherit a seat of honor. (V. 8)

Once again, a great reversal is being described. Mighty warriors no longer have instruments of warfare; their bows are broken and they have become weak, whereas those who were weak
receive strength. The rich, who had food enough and to spare,
will work all day for a single crust of bread, while the ones who
were starving will starve no more.

The good news to the poor and needy is spelled out in verse
8: those who have dwelt in dust and ashes (those whom Frantz

Fanon called "the wretched of the earth") will grovel no more in their poverty; they will consort with the high and mighty and find their rightful places there. The imagery is consistently spatial: those who were on top will be on the bottom, those who were on the bottom will be on top.

It's not a message calculated to soothe bureaucrats, who want things to continue running smoothly just as they always have (thanks to the bureaucrats, as they will be the first to tell us). But if you are feeble and hungry and down somewhere in the ash heap, it might just be the best news that ever came down the pike.

These two women, Hannah and Mary, have provided a charter for revolution, articulating themes that men—those valiant defenders of the status quo—successfully kept submerged for the centuries that separated the two singers. But revolutionary ideas have a habit of not staying submerged. They reappear. They have reappeared in our day wherever the poor are beginning to hear good news once again.

Take Latin America. . . .

ITEMS FOR REFLECTION AND DISCUSSION

In Latin America, there are few biblical passages more widely used than Mary's song. In the light of our textual study, it seems likely that Christians there have heard the words more accurately than we have, and that the best thing we can do is try to listen to what they hear. So the remainder of this chapter will simply describe three episodes that can open up Mary's song to us in new ways.

1. "The Mass is ended."

With these words, spoken in Spanish by the celebrant, several thousand worshipers get to their feet, preparing to leave the assembly hall. They have been at a "summer course" in Lima, Peru, offered for people who want to see how theology and Scripture and Catholic spirituality can be means for overcoming the poverty and oppression and injustice that characterize the villages to which they will return. As they leave the hall, they start singing. And what are they singing? Mary's song. My wife and I are there, strangers to the culture and partway strangers even to the language. The words they are singing are familiar; we share, after all, the same Scriptures. But on another level the words are brand-new, never before heard by either of us. For on the lips of poor and oppressed people, the words are transformed from the whispers of a dutiful maiden into the promise of a wide-scale victory soon to be achieved.

Those who have every reason to wonder whether God can any longer be called a God of justice and power are singing, *"God has shown strength with God's arm."*

Those who have so often been victimized by arrogant rulers who show no regard for the poor are singing, *"God has scattered the proud in the imagination of their hearts."*

Those who have been threatened and imprisoned by leaders whose grip on power seems secure are singing, *"God has put down the mighty from their thrones."*

Those who have seen their families ground down and destroyed, with no apparent hope of ever rising again, are singing, *"God has exalted those of low degree."*

Those who worry about food for themselves and their children are singing, *"God has filled the hungry with good things."*

Those from whom the rich take more and more, whether legally or illegally, are singing, *"And the rich God has sent empty away."*

They are singing of a new order, a new world in which all expectations have been turned around. Those in power have their spies and informers inside the meeting, of course, and their army (in the guise of the police) outside the meeting. Surely the police, hearing such revolutionary slogans as "Put down the mighty from their thrones!" and "Exalt those of low degree!" should have their guns at the ready as the crowd leaves the assembly hall.

But the crowd understands the wisdom of the serpent as well
as the gentleness of the dove. For what can the police, "good
Catholics" all, do? All the worshipers are doing is singing a
prayer song by a dutiful, demure little Jewish girl who just
happens, as far as those in Lima, Peru, are concerned, to be the
Mother of the Lord Jesus Christ and the Queen of Heaven.

2. In Ernesto Cardenal's *The Gospel in Solentiname,* a collec-
tion of comments on Gospel passages by members of the fishing
community in Solentiname, Nicaragua, the following exchange
takes place during a discussion of Mary's song:

> I asked what they thought Herod would have said if he
> had known that a woman of the people had sung that God
> had pulled down the mighty and raised up the humble,
> filled the hungry with good things and left the rich with
> nothing.
>   Natalia laughed and said: "He'd say she was crazy."
>   Rosita: "That she was a communist."
>
> (Vol. 1, pp. 30–31)

What would you call Mary? Would you agree with Natalia or
Rosita or both? And how would you handle the even more
provocative comment by Laureano: "The point isn't that they
would just *say* the Virgin was a communist. She *was* a communist" (p. 31).

3. In a South American country where there has been great
persecution of church leaders, a number of priests have cast
their lot with the poor, living in the slum area of a large city,
working at whatever jobs (street sweeping, housepainting) will
pay for food and rent, and conducting informal Sunday "litur-
gies" at which the people comment on events of the week, and
the priests relate those events to appropriate biblical passages.
One such exchange went like this:

> PRIEST: Today is September 12. Does that date mean
> anything special to you?
>   RESPONSE: Three years ago yesterday Allende was killed

in Chile and the Chileans lost their leader. Now they are suffering repression.

RESPONSE: Allende's death makes me think of the death of Martin Luther King.

PRIEST: Why do you think of the deaths of those two together?

RESPONSE: Because both of them were concerned about oppressed peoples.

PRIEST: Doesn't the day mean anything but *death* to you?

RESPONSE: Well, today is also the Feast of the Holy Name of Mary. So this day also makes me think of her.

PRIEST: Is there any connection between Allende and Martin Luther King and Mary?

RESPONSE: I guess that would depend on whether Mary was concerned about oppressed peoples too.

PRIEST: Let me read part of Mary's song, the Magnificat, in the beginning of Luke's Gospel: "God has scattered the proud in the imagination of their hearts, put down the mighty from their thrones, and exalted those of low degree; has filled the hungry with good things, and the rich has sent empty away."

RESPONSE: Bravo! But, Father, that doesn't sound at all like the Mary we hear about in the cathedral. And the Mary in the "holy pictures" certainly doesn't look like a person who would talk that way.

PRIEST: Tell us about the Mary in the holy pictures.

RESPONSE *(displaying a picture):* Here she is. She is standing on a crescent moon. She is wearing a crown. She has rings on her fingers. She has a blue robe embroidered with gold.

PRIEST: That *does* sound like a different Mary from the Mary of the song! Do you think the picture has betrayed the Mary of the song?

RESPONSE: The Mary who said that God "has exalted those of low degree" would not have left all of her friends so she could stand on the moon.

CORPORATE RESPONSE: Take her off the moon!

RESPONSE: The Mary who said that God "has put down the mighty from their thrones" would not be wearing a crown.

CORPORATE RESPONSE: Take off her crown!

RESPONSE: The Mary who said that God "has sent the rich empty away" would not be wearing rings on her fingers.

CORPORATE RESPONSE: Take off her rings!

RESPONSE: The Mary who said that God has "filled the hungry with good things" would not have left people who were still hungry to wear a silk robe embroidered with gold.

CORPORATE RESPONSE: Take off her robe!

ANGUISHED RESPONSE: But, Father, this is not right! *(embarrassedly)* We're—we're doing a striptease of the Virgin.

PRIEST: Very well. If you don't like the way Mary looks in *this* picture, what do you think the Mary of the song would look like?

RESPONSE: The Mary of the song would not be standing on the moon. She would be standing in the dirt and dust where we stand.

RESPONSE: The Mary of the song would not be wearing a crown. She would have on an old hat like the rest of us, to keep the sun from causing her to faint.

RESPONSE: The Mary of the song would not be wearing jeweled rings on her fingers. She would have rough hands like ours.

RESPONSE: The Mary of the song would not be wearing a silk robe embroidered with gold. She would be wearing old clothes like the rest of us.

EMBARRASSED RESPONSE: Father, it may be awful to say this, but it sounds as though Mary would look just like me! My feet are dirty, my hat is old, my hands are rough, and my clothes are torn.

PRIEST: No, I don't think it is awful to say that. I think the Mary you have all described is more like the Mary of the Bible than the Mary we hear about in the cathedral and see in all the holy pictures.

RESPONSE: I think she'd be more at home here in the slum with us than in the cathedral or the General's Mansion.

RESPONSE: I think her message is more hopeful for us than for them. They are mighty and rich, but she tells them that God puts down the mighty from their thrones and sends the rich away empty.

RESPONSE: And we are at the bottom of the heap and very hungry, but she tells us that God exalts those of low degree and fills the hungry with good things.

PRIEST: Now let's see, how could we begin to help God bring those things to pass?

6. JESUS AT NAZARETH:
"GOOD NEWS TO THE POOR"
(Changing Structures)

Luke 4:16–30

We are discovering that the Bible says a great deal about "the poor." Sometimes it seems as though the message is so exclusively for the poor that the rest of us are either ignored or castigated, fifth-round draft choices at best.

It all seems askew, for while the poor do get a lot of attention in the Bible, the nonpoor get a lot of attention in the church and usually end up running things. One reason for this is that the nonpoor have become the official interpreters of the Scriptures and have managed to take most of the sting out of passages dealing with the poor. Luke's blunt talk about "the poor," we are instructed, must be interpreted in the light of Matthew's fuller "poor *in spirit,*" a classification to which we can all aspire, since it has none of the rude realities of "material poverty" (lack of food, clothing, shelter, employment) attached to it. "Spiritual poverty" in fact becomes a Christian virtue, and we are encouraged to affirm a life-style that puts no premium on goods and possessions but equally does not suggest that we need to get rid of them. It's all a matter of attitude. . . .

The more we press this kind of logic—as the church has done with consummate skill for centuries—the less threatening the Bible becomes. If people can be "poor in spirit" whether materially wealthy or materially deprived, then we can concentrate on the "inner" life and keep the gospel insulated from such aspects of "outer" life as the nature of the economic order, the equitable sharing of the world's goods, or the need to care for the indigent. We have looked at passages in the Hebrew Scriptures that challenge this conclusion. But the conclusion is picked up in the Christian Scriptures as well. If the exodus is the paradigm story for the Hebrew Scriptures, the episode in the synagogue in Nazareth is the paradigm story for the Christian Scriptures. No passage is more consistently referred to by third world Christians than this one—and no wonder, since in it Jesus issues an unequivocal challenge to the ways we "spiritualize" his message.

THE BIBLICAL TEXT: LUKE 4:16–30

[16]And he came to Nazareth, where he had been brought up; and he went to the synagogue, as his custom was, on the sabbath day. And he stood up to read; [17]and there was given to him the book of the prophet Isaiah. He opened the book, and found the place where it was written,
> [18]"The Spirit of the Lord is upon me,
> because he has anointed me to preach good news
>   to the poor.
> He has sent me to proclaim release to the captives
> and recovering of sight to the blind,
> to set at liberty those who are oppressed,
> [19]to proclaim the acceptable year of the Lord."

[20]And he closed the book, and gave it back to the attendant, and sat down; and the eyes of all in the synagogue were fixed on him. [21]And he began to say to them, "Today this scripture has been fulfilled in your hearing." [22]And all spoke well of him, and wondered at the gracious words which proceeded out of his mouth; and they said, "Is not this Joseph's son?" [23]And he said to them, "Doubtless you will quote to me this proverb, 'Physician, heal yourself; what we have heard you did at Capernaum, do here also in your own country.' " [24]And he said, "Truly, I say to

you, no prophet is acceptable in his own country. ²⁵But in truth, I tell you, there were many widows in Israel in the days of Elijah, when the heaven was shut up three years and six months, when there came a great famine over all the land; ²⁶and Elijah was sent to none of them but only to Zarephath, in the land of Sidon, to a woman who was a widow. ²⁷And there were many lepers in Israel in the time of the prophet Elisha; and none of them was cleansed, but only Naaman the Syrian." ²⁸When they heard this, all in the synagogue were filled with wrath. ²⁹And they rose up and put him out of the city, and led him to the brow of the hill on which their city was built, that they might throw him down headlong. ³⁰But passing through the midst of them he went away.

The episode seems tame enough—an account of Sabbath worship in a small-town synagogue. It's hardly the stuff of high drama. And yet the scene that starts in tranquillity comes to its climax in an attempt to lynch the guest speaker.

The hometown boy is back home. He has been away for a while, doing nobody-is-quite-sure-what, save that it certainly wasn't bulk purchasing for the carpenter's shop where he works with his father. No matter, here he is safe and sound, sitting in the family pew, just like old times.

So they ask him to read the Scripture lesson. It's a familiar passage, Isaiah 61, full of hope and promise, a passage most of the hearers know by heart, and tonight the words come through with new beauty, for he reads them very well indeed. When he has finished, he gives the scroll back to the attendant and comments that the words they have just heard are coming true right now.

The hearers are charmed. Such eloquence! Such clarity of diction! Such self-possession! Such a clear, well-modulated voice! A few who had lost touch with the family come to their senses with a shock of recognition. "Isn't that Joe's boy?" they ask, and sure enough, it is—the kid from down the block, little

Joshua, grown up now and making such a fine impression. How proud his mother must be. One of them catches her eye and she looks away, blushing with pleasure at the recognition accorded her eldest son.

And then Joshua (or, as we would say, Jesus), not knowing enough to quit while he's ahead, starts explaining things. It's a tactical blunder. He is almost defensive about the warm reception, and he tells about times of famine and illness in the past, when a divine visitation was expected, and when God did indeed come, but not to the folk who were waiting eagerly but to a bunch of outsiders.

As Jesus develops these unwelcome thoughts, the spell he cast is broken. The temperature in the synagogue drops well below freezing. What kind of talk is this? Who does this young upstart thing he is to tell us that the nonbelievers, the people who are sitting at home watching TV instead of coming to church, are of more concern to God than those of us who show up regularly (at considerable inconvenience, we might add) to honor God's name? Is *that* what he thinks those memorable words in Isaiah are all about? Heresy. Abomination. So the temperature rapidly shoots up past the boiling point. As Clarence Jordan translates the verse describing the people's reaction, "When they heard that, the whole congregation blew a gasket" (*The Cotton Patch Version of Luke and Acts,* p. 25).

The story literally becomes a cliff-hanger. The irate listeners hustle Jesus out of the synagogue, and all of them jostle their way to the top of one of those high hills surrounding Nazareth. They have a plan: they are going to swing him three times out over the steepest cliff they can find and let go on the third swing. So much for hometown boys who come back and try to tell off their elders.

Somehow, perhaps because of the darkness and overall confusion, Jesus gets away, and there is no lynching that night. But instead of learning from the experience, he obstinately continues to preach the same disturbing message elsewhere. A couple of years later another mob gets its hands on him, takes him to another hill outside another city, and makes sure this time that he doesn't get away.

OTHER BIBLICAL PASSAGES

Three passages need attention.

1. Isaiah 61:1–2 is the Scripture Jesus reads. The wording of Isaiah's and Luke's versions are virtually identical, as we can see by placing them side by side:

Isaiah 61:1–2	*Luke 4:18–19*
The Spirit of the Lord GOD is upon me,	The Spirit of the Lord is upon me,
because the LORD has anointed me to bring good tidings to the afflicted;	because he has anointed me to preach good news to the poor.
he has sent me to bind up the brokenhearted,	He has sent me
to proclaim liberty to the captives,	to proclaim release to the captives
	and recovering of sight to the blind,
and the opening of the prison to those who are bound;	to set at liberty those who are oppressed,
to proclaim the year of the LORD'S favor.	to proclaim the acceptable year of the Lord.

The full Isaiah passage is an eleven-verse poem. The poem as a whole makes even more prominent a theme apparent in the quoted portions—the theme of *reversal,* celebrating the fact that things are getting turned around, and offering hope to those who had had no reason to hope. Individuals who mourn will be given "a *garland* [symbol of rejoicing] instead of ashes [symbol of sadness], the oil of *gladness* instead of mourning, the mantle of

praise instead of a faint spirit" (Isa. 61:3, italics added).
Similar reversals will take place on a social scale too:

> They shall *build up* the ancient ruins,
>   they shall *raise up* the former devastations;
> they shall *repair* the ruined cities,
>   the devastations of many generations.
>   (Isa. 61:4, italics added)

This simply highlights the prominence of the theme of social
reversal in the portions Jesus quotes: the *poor,* whose lives have
been one succession after another of bad news, will get good
news; the *captives,* whose lives have consisted of being bound,
will be released; the *blind,* who have been denied sight, will see
again; and the *oppressed,* whose lives have been nothing but
enslavement, will be freed, or (in the word used today) liberated.
Everything is reversed.

2. Can this single passage be made the focal point of Jesus'
whole message, as third world Christians insist? Let us compare
it with another summary of his message. John the Baptist, in
prison for pricking the vanity of the ruler, sends messengers to
Jesus to find out what he is up to. Matthew and Luke record
Jesus' response in almost identical words. The similarity of
language suggests that both writers had access to a document
of an earlier date than either gospel.

Matthew 11:4–5	*Luke 7:22*
Go and tell John what you hear and see: the blind receive their sight and the lame walk, lepers are cleansed and the deaf hear, and the dead are raised up, and the poor have good news preached to them.	Go and tell John what you have seen and heard: the blind receive their sight, the lame walk, lepers are cleansed, and the deaf hear, the dead are raised up, the poor have good news preached to them.

The striking convergence between these summaries and
the message at Nazareth should dispel any doubt that we are

close to the core of Jesus' message.

3. Another biblical passage is crucial to our understanding of what is going on in the synagogue, alluded to when Jesus closes off the reading with Isaiah's reference to "the acceptable year of the Lord." A nice homiletical conclusion, a phrase one can roll around on the tongue—also one of the biggest con jobs in the history of translation.

For what does "the acceptable year of the Lord" mean? It means "the Jubilee year." And what does the Jubilee year mean? Leviticus 25:1–24 provides a full answer, and it will help us understand why tumult breaks out in the synagogue, and why the authorities in Jerusalem were after Jesus almost as soon as he had eluded the folks in Nazareth.

Just as persons are supposed to rest every seventh day, the Sabbath, so the earth is supposed to rest every seventh year.

> In the seventh year there shall be a sabbath of solemn rest
> for the land, a sabbath to the Lord; you shall not sow your
> field or prune your vineyard. (Lev. 25:4)

Since this could threaten the economic survival of farmers and vintners, God promises that the sixth-year crops will be sufficient to tide people over the seventh year.

After seven cycles of "sabbatical" years comes the fiftieth year, called the Jubilee year. A Jubilee year is a sabbatical year on a grand scale; "scope" is a word that comes to mind. Four characteristics stand out (for details see Yoder, *The Politics of Jesus,* pp. 34–40, 64–67):

1. As with the regular sabbatical year, *the soil is to lie fallow.*

2. *Debts are to be canceled.* (The phrase in the Lord's Prayer "Forgive us our debts as we forgive our debtors" is what the year of Jubilee enjoins.) Everybody gets a fresh start. The Lord's Prayer is a great Jubilee prayer.

3. *Slaves are to be freed.* The Jubilee injunction "Proclaim liberty throughout the land to *all* its inhabitants" (Lev. 25:10, emphasis added) means exactly what it says, and the phrase

"liberty to the captives," in both Isaiah and Luke, is an echo of the Jubilee command. At least once in Israel's history a freeing of slaves actually took place. On this occasion, Yahweh commended the Israelites: "Today you have repented and have done what is pleasing in my sight, each one proclaiming liberation for all human beings" (Jer. 34:15). But the breakthrough was short-lived. Yahweh had to continue, "But then you changed your minds again and you profaned my name to re-enslave each one" (Jer. 34:16). Freeing slaves is too costly to the economy.

4. And, speaking of the economy: *Capital is to be redistributed.* In Israel's agrarian society, the Jubilee year provides that land acquired since the previous Jubilee shall revert to its former owners. Whatever inequities have accumulated in the interval will be set right in this fashion; people cannot accumulate inordinate amounts of land at the expense of others. Overriding reason: the land is not theirs but Yahweh's. "The land shall not be sold in perpetuity," Yahweh says, "for the land is mine" (Lev. 25:23).

This, then, is the not-so-innocuous "acceptable year of the Lord." Jesus proclaims that it is *now* coming to pass, and he identifies it as central to his message. We need not be concerned with every detail of the Jubilee year, nor even with the question of how often (if ever) it was actually observed. The important thing is the *nature* of the Jubilee, which is a program for radical social change. No one who takes the Jubilee seriously can accuse Jesus of preaching only a "spiritual," individualistic message. The Jubilee emphasis means that Jesus' mission is "a visible socio-political-economic restructuring of relations among the people of God" (Yoder, *The Politics of Jesus,* p. 39). The message is shatteringly direct: the good news is for the poor and oppressed; it is liberation from bondage, whether the bondage is political, economic, social, or all three. Debts will be canceled, slavery will be annulled, vast land holdings will be broken up. Everything will be restructured.

ITEMS FOR REFLECTION AND DISCUSSION

Let us highlight five items:

1. *Why did Jesus' hearers react so violently?* To answer this
question, let us ask another: Who is most threatened by a reversal of the way things are? Answer: those who have it made under
existing arrangements and therefore *like* the way things are.
They can be counted on to resist proposals for change.

Who is most threatened if prisoners are freed? Answer: the
jailers, who will not only lose their jobs but may even lose their
lives if the released inmates are sufficiently resentful of their
treatment during incarceration.

Who is most threatened if oppressed peoples are liberated?
Answer: the oppressors who have built their own prosperity out
of the exploitation of others.

It is the *beneficiaries* of an economic system, a political structure, or a religious establishment who are most threatened by
change, most perturbed by talk of "reversal," most inclined to
silence such talk and exterminate such speakers. This is true
whether they have deliberately sought to oppress or are merely
the compliant recipients of the benefits of oppressive actions by
others.

And who are most excited by the news that things could be
different? Answer: *the victims* of the economic system, political
structure, or religious establishment, those whom such systems
have ground down and tried to destroy.

2. The heart of Jesus' message is unambiguous: *"good news to
the poor."* It is the theme in Luke 7, Matthew 11, Isaiah 61, and
dozens of similar passages in addition to the one we are studying. Those of us who are not poor have to confront that reality.
It is difficult to do so, for there is another question: Who stands
to lose if there is "good news to the poor"? Answer: the nonpoor, or, less euphemistically, the rich. If reversals are the order
of the day, that means that if the poor are no longer poor, then

the rich will no longer be rich. And who among the rich wants that? So, as already hinted, we "spiritualize" the meaning of "the poor."

Northern hemisphere commentaries on these verses furnish a dreary litany of examples. The term "the poor" is to be understood in an "inward, spiritual sense." Those described as "captive, blind, oppressed" are victims of "inward repressions, neuroses, and other spiritual ills." "Captivity" has nothing to do with persons in real jails; it means "the inward but terribly real imprisonment into which their souls may fall." When "the poor" are mentioned in the Beatitudes, "Jesus lays *all* the emphasis on the spiritual or inward character of redemption." (See my *Theology in a New Key,* pp. 82–84, for other examples.)

When we listen to third world peoples interpreting biblical treatments of the poor, one fact stands out: "spiritual" interpretations won't wash. An exegetical study of words for "the poor," such as Elsa Tamez, the Costa Rican biblical scholar, has conducted, demonstrates that "when Jesus reads the promise now fulfilled in him, 'He anointed me to preach good news to the poor,' he is referring to all those who lack the basic necessities of life. When he says, 'Blessed are you poor' (Luke 6:20), he is referring to material poverty."

> The poor in the Bible are the helpless, the indigent, the hungry, the oppressed, the needy, the humiliated. And it is not nature that has put them in this situation; they have been unjustly impoverished and despoiled by the powerful. (Tamez, *Bible of the Oppressed,* p. 70)

To what kind of analysis does this interpretation lead? Gustavo Gutiérrez helps us work this through (see *A Theology of Liberation,* especially chapter 13, "Poverty, Solidarity and Protest"). Against all attempts to transform poverty into the "spiritual poverty" referred to earlier, he stresses the brute reality of *material poverty,* lack of sufficient economic goods to lead a full human life, which describes perhaps 70 percent of the

human family. Recognition that material poverty is unequivo-
cally evil is the bottom line. Gutiérrez' threefold distinction
drawn in *A Theology of Liberation* reinforces the conclusions of
Elsa Tamez:

a. "Poverty is a scandalous condition inimical to human
dignity and therefore contrary to the will of God" (p. 291).
English equivalents to the Hebrew words for "the poor" are
such things as the frail one, the weak one, the bent-over one, the
humiliated one. The New Testament Greek word *ptōchos* means
"one who does not have what is necessary to subsist" and is
forced into the degrading activity of begging. Furthermore, as
Gutiérrez and Tamez both emphasize, those who are poor are
poor not through their own fault or because of fate but because
of the injustice of the oppressors, who "grind the heads of the
poor into the earth, and thrust the humble out of their way"
(Amos 2:7). Throughout the Scriptures, this kind of poverty *and
the social conditions that cause it* are condemned. The Jubilee
year was a conscious attempt to restructure social conditions to
get rid of such injustice and poverty.

b. There is also a biblical concept of poverty as "spiritual
childhood," trust in God, a willingness not to rely on material
security but to be totally available for God.

c. The most complete biblical understanding of poverty is a
melding of *(a)* and *(b)*, involving *solidarity with the poor* and
protest against poverty. One does not accept poverty as good; one
opposes it by commitment to, and alignment with, its victims.
Sharing material goods in the early church was not "a question
of erecting poverty as an ideal, but rather of seeing to it that
there were no poor" (p. 301).

3. If that is indeed the biblical message, *how do we respond?*
In the Roman Catholic Church in Latin America, which lives
in the midst of a poverty the rest of us cannot imagine, the
bishops (not just far-out priests and laypeople but the bishops)
concluded at their conference in Puebla, Mexico, in 1979 that
the church must make "a preferential option for the poor." Its

primary concern must be to minister to, and work with, the materially poor.

What does this mean, and how do we respond?

a. The option is "preferential," not exclusive. It does not mean lack of concern for the nonpoor; it does mean that concern for the nonpoor must be dealt with in the context of concern for the poor, *and not the other way around,* which is more radical than it sounds on first hearing.

b. The bishops also dedicated the church to "a preferential option for youth." Since the most appalling victims of poverty are children, the two preferential options are complementary. The phrase *Y los únicos privilegiados serán los niños* ("And the only privileged ones will be the children") captures the complementarity and is not a bad description of the kingdom of God.

c. An *immediate* "preferential option for the poor" is the way to an *ultimate* option for all. To opt for the poor is not only to say that they should not be poor but to challenge whatever or whoever perpetuates their poverty. If we participate (as we do) in structures that oppress others, we must either change those structures or break with them, and if we try to perpetuate them, others must render us incapable of doing so. This will work for our own salvation as well as that of the victims, since in dehumanizing others we dehumanize ourselves as well. We may fear the social surgery that such change demands, but the consequences for us, too, will finally be beneficial: if no one can any longer oppress and destroy, that is good news for everyone.

4. Jesus seems intent on adding insult to injury. Not only does he say in the synagogue that the poor are the recipients of the good news, which excludes most of his listeners; he also says that the outcasts, nonreligious types, and people from other nations and cultures get preferential treatment, which excludes the rest of them. It is the Jubilee message and the Isaiah message pushed to the limit. And in the dynamics of the evening, this is what really upsets them.

Jesus begins with the self-fulfilling prophecy that "no prophet is acceptable in his own country" (Luke 4:24) and for the rest of the evening proceeds to demonstrate his own nonacceptability. All he does is tell two stories—the Nathan syndrome at work again—reminding them of well-recorded but not well-remembered episodes. "Remember that famine back in the days of Elijah?" he asks. "There were a lot of widows in Israel at that time, but Elijah, our own Israelite prophet, disregarded them to comfort a woman in Sidon, a foreign country." That produces quite a few gasps and costs him the women's vote: doesn't God care about the women of *our* nation, which after all is God's nation?

But Jesus isn't finished. There is a story for the men as well. "Remember that terrible epidemic of leprosy back in the days of Elisha? There were a lot of lepers in Israel at that time, but Elisha, our own Israelite prophet, went to none of them. Instead, he cured an enemy army commander, a foreigner, an outsider, a Syrian, no less—that brutal Naaman, who once slaughtered a whole camel caravan for straying outside of its assigned territory." That produces some more gasps and completes the alienation of whatever men are still there.

The offense is clear. Jesus is making the untidy suggestion that there is no necessary connection between worshiping in the synagogue and receiving God's favor. Being an Israelite or a Southern Baptist is no guarantee that God's benefits will first of all (if ever) come to you; on the divine scoreboard, the last may be first and the first last—which is, to say the least, a rotten way to keep score and a real put-down to piety and good intentions. It is gasket-blowing time.

5. Jesus' message is *both old and new.* We need both affirmations.

On the one hand, it is not a message he whips up on the spur of the moment when the beadle (after a whispered conversation with the president of the synagogue) taps Jesus on the shoulder and asks if he would care to read the lesson and say a few words.

Isaiah 61 is a well-known part of the prophetic heritage, and Jesus positions himself squarely within it. Furthermore, there is a divine authentication stamped on the words. Jesus does not begin, "While I've been out of town I've had a few thoughts I'd like to share, and then I'll get your reactions during the coffee hour." Instead, he straightforwardly identifies with Isaiah's words, saying, "The Spirit of the Lord is upon me," which is about as much divine authentication as anyone could hope for. And the authentication is intensely specific. *Why* is "the Spirit of the Lord" upon him? Because, Jesus tells us, "[the Spirit of the Lord] has anointed me to *preach good news to the poor.*" That is what the Spirit of the Lord is all about: the poor, the captives, the oppressed—as recipients, all, of the Jubilee promises. A new idea, this linking of God with the cause of the oppressed? No. Old stuff. Been around for centuries. Time to start taking it seriously.

And that is where the new comes in. For as soon as Jesus finishes reading, he announces that the message is no longer a dream for the future. His comment is not "Someday, God willing, this scripture will be fulfilled, perhaps even in the hearing of your grandchildren," but *"Today* this scripture *has been fulfilled* in *your* hearing" (Luke 4:21). No room for misunderstanding in *that* declaration.

The congregation nevertheless misunderstands at first, and there is all the talk about the clear, well-modulated voice. Not until Jesus makes those unsettling comments about the widow of Zarephath and Naaman the Syrian do his listeners really begin to hear him. They don't like what they hear. "You mean we are supposed to be open to *everybody,* right *now,* and *change* things that make it hard to do that?"

Let us hear the message once more, as nakedly as possible, from this new perspective:

> The land is not to be exploited any more, slaves are to be freed, debts are to be canceled, capital unjustly gained is

to be redistributed. Any political, economic, social, or religious structures that perpetuate exploitation must be changed to create a society committed to the reversal of the plight of the poor (meaning the materially poor), the captives (meaning the dregs), the blind (meaning the blind), and the oppressed (meaning the victims). The provisions of the Jubilee are not spiritual consolation prizes for those who fail to make it here and now, they are specific descriptions of what the here and now is *already* in process of becoming.

The "Jesus movement," as Clarence Jordan calls the church, is dedicated to bringing about this kind of change. If you don't think so, ask Herod or Pilate, both of whom were smart enough to understand what an unacceptable threat Jesus posed. Between them they had enough political and military clout to finish the job the synagogue crowd botched.

Or so they thought.

On the basis of the foregoing, here are a few exercises:

• Since this passage talks about *restructuring* political, economic, and social life, what does this say about involvement in our political parties, our economic system, our residential patterns? Are Christians supposed to engage in frontal assaults or work for gradual transformation from within? Would the strategies of Christians differ in *(a)* a small Latin American country run by a U.S.-supported dictator, *(b)* a world power run along dictatorial lines with widespread secret police, and *(c)* a country with liberties for the well-to-do but lack of economic opportunity for the poor?

• What are modern counterparts to Jesus' assertion that strangers and foreigners (Sidonians, Syrians) may be the recipients of God's compassion before the religious folk? If the man who slaughtered a camel caravan for straying off course is of special concern to God, what might this mean for those who ordered the shooting down of a Korean commercial airliner that strayed over forbidden territory?

• Could contemporary society hold together if the Jubilee year were reintroduced? What features of it are transferable to our world? (Would you answer the question differently if you had no job, food, land, or shelter?)

• For forty years the Somoza family in Nicaragua systematically expropriated farmland belonging to peasants. (Since one member of the family was the U.S.-backed dictator of Nicaragua, this was not particularly difficult.) When Somoza was overthrown and the Sandinistas came to power, they began restoring plots of land to the former owners. (So great had the Somoza landholdings become that if all their land had been redistributed across the board, every peasant family in Nicaragua would have gotten five acres.) A number of peasants who were Christians compared the recovery of their ancestral lands to the fulfillment of the promises of the Jubilee year. Does this seem to you an appropriate reaction?

• Is a "preferential option for the poor" really compatible with a belief that God loves *all* people?

• Can comfort and well-being stand in the way of doing the will of God? Consider the unlikely line in Hugh T. Kerr's hymn "God of Our Life": "When we are *strong*, Lord, leave us not alone."

7. JESUS' STORY:
FROM HEAD TRIPS TO FOOT TRIPS
(Changing the Question)

Luke 10:25–37

No story Jesus ever told is more familiar than the parable of the good Samaritan. And yet its very popularity poses a problem; the overfamiliar tends to slide by us. When the morning Scripture lesson begins "A man was going down from Jerusalem to Jericho . . ." we can tune out. We know what comes next.

Our third world friends have helped to shake us out of our conventional ways of dealing with the Bible, and their approach to this story is no exception. We see the story as a way of answering a question. And what they are pointing out to us is that in the course of the episode *the question changes.* When the questions change, the answers change too.

There is a question shift in this story about neighborliness, which suggests that our answer to what it means to be a neighbor may have to shift also.

Because this is the most popular of Jesus' parables, it has been the object of intensive critical attention. Indeed, as the whole literary genre of parable has been reexamined in recent years, this parable has often been reduced to a few verses and stripped from its surrounding context. For our discussion, however, we will assume the unity of the passage (Luke 10: 25–37) and deal not only with the parable itself but also with the circumstances that produced it and the new circumstances it produced.

THE BIBLICAL TEXT: LUKE 10:25–37

> [25]And behold, a lawyer stood up to put him to the
> test, saying, "Teacher, what shall I do to inherit eternal
> life?" [26]He said to him, "What is written in the law? How
> do you read?" [27]And he answered, "You shall love the
> Lord your God with all your heart, and with all your soul,
> and with all your strength, and with all your mind; and
> your neighbor as yourself." [28]And he said to him, "You
> have answered right; do this, and you will live."
> [29]But he, desiring to justify himself, said to Jesus,
> "And who is my neighbor?" [30]Jesus replied, "A man was
> going down from Jerusalem to Jericho, and he fell among
> robbers, who stripped him and beat him, and departed,
> leaving him half dead. [31]Now by chance a priest was going
> down that road; and when he saw him he passed by on the
> other side. [32]So likewise a Levite, when he came to the
> place and saw him, passed by on the other side. [33]But a
> Samaritan, as he journeyed, came to where he was; and
> when he saw him, he had compassion, [34]and went to him
> and bound up his wounds, pouring on oil and wine; then
> he set him on his own beast and brought him to an inn,
> and took care of him. [35]And the next day he took out two
> denarii and gave them to the innkeeper, saying, 'Take care
> of him; and whatever more you spend, I will repay you
> when I come back.' [36]Which of these three, do you think,
> proved neighbor to the man who fell among the robbers?"
> [37]He said, "The one who showed mercy on him." And
> Jesus said to him, "Go and do likewise."

The situation is a familiar one in Jesus' ministry: some
clever questioners are trying to trap him. A lawyer, possessing
a Doctor of Jurisprudence degree from a first-rate law school
where he also edited the Law Review, along with a Ph.D. in
Humanities that he picked up along the way, has a question:
what shall he do to inherit eternal life? Jesus, in good pedagog-

ical fashion, throws the question back to him and elicits the response that eternal life involves loving God and loving one's neighbor. Jesus tells him to get on with it, since he now knows what to do, but the lawyer, unwilling to be disposed of so easily, reenters the fray. He has another question: "Who is my neighbor?"

By asking the question that way, the lawyer gets the discussion back onto safe territory. The discussion need not involve *being* a neighbor but only *defining* a neighbor. An academic exploration can ensue, and the lawyer, his own life-style now exempt from scrutiny, can do brilliantly in the ensuing verbal exchange. It is the kind of terrain on which lawyers excel.

Let us explore the lawyer's inner reflections: should the discussion prove fruitful, perhaps a symposium can be organized around a theme like "The Concept of Neighborliness" and a really comprehensive definition arrived at. The lawyer, in fact, sits on the board of a small foundation that might be persuaded to finance such a project. There could be a series of papers: "The Stoic Concept of Neighborliness," "Neighborliness in Recent Mid-East Fiction" (a very short paper), "The Cultural Implications of Neighborliness for Improving Trade Relations with Greece," "Neighborliness: A Woman's Perspective" (written by a man in order to maintain the desired objectivity), and finally, tapping the local Ph.D. thesis market, "Neighborliness as Seen by Members of the Slave Class, Being a Series of Interviews Conducted in the Alexandrian Slave Market for the Purpose of Attaining Contemporary Data on Satisfaction/Dissatisfaction Ratios." The papers (the lawyer continues to reflect) could then be published, perhaps edited by the lawyer himself, and the contributors could add the volume to their list of publications as a way of assuring that they get academic tenure—rather than their neighbors.

The fantasy (which I regret to report is far from fanciful) illustrates the skill with which we use thought to avoid action. A classic ploy.

And Jesus cuts right through it. He refuses to play academic games. He tells a story.

There is surely no better way to put down a Ph.D.: "A story? I thought we were going to have a stimulating intellectual discussion, and he tells stories." Even so, the lawyer has to listen. After all, he asked the question, and if he wants to know Jesus' answer, he'll have to see what kind of definition he can extract from the story.

An undocumented worker (Jesus begins) was walking down from Nob Hill to Fisherman's Wharf. On the way, a bunch of teen-age addicts, desperate for a fix, grabbed his wallet, beat him up, and left him in the gutter, half dead. Now by chance a Presbyterian minister was going down the same street, but when he saw the man he crossed over to the other side at the traffic light, since he was already late for a board meeting. The executive vice-president of the San Francisco Social Service Agency, when he came to the place and saw him, also crossed over to the other side; he was collecting his thoughts for a speech on "Remedies for Juvenile Delinquency" that he was about to give at a prayer luncheon. Then a clerk from the Russian embassy drove by, and when she came to the place where the man lay, she had compassion on him, and taking the first-aid kit from the glove compartment, she stopped her car and tried to bind up the man's wounds. She then put him in the back seat of the car, getting blood all over the upholstery, and drove him to Mercy Hospital. Since the victim had no Blue Cross coverage and the hospital would not admit him without a financially reliable sponsor, the young Russian took out her purse, gave the admitting clerk two fifty-dollar bills, and said, "Take care of him; and if this isn't enough, here is my VISA credit card. We can settle the difference when I return tomorrow."

We will look at the story in two ways: first in terms of the lawyer's question and then in terms of Jesus' new question.

1. Let us be sure we have registered the shock value that is communicated by the story's traditional title, "The Good Sa-

maritan." In Jesus' day, one simply could not juxtapose the adjective "good" with the noun "Samaritan," for that would have produced the combination "good Samaritan," and to Jesus' hearers that was unthinkable, for Samaritans were, by definition, evil; they were the enemy. In like fashion, many people in our society cannot conceive of juxtaposing the adjective "good" and the noun "Russian," for that would produce the combination "good Russian," which is unthinkable, for Russians are, by definition, evil; they are the enemy. The notion that a godlessatheistcommunistrussian would be moved by "compassion" (which we know is an American, not a Russian, trait) is also unthinkable, and the notion that a godlessatheistcommunistrussian would emerge as morally superior to a Protestant minister or the head of a social service agency is nothing but communist propaganda.

If the Russian analogy doesn't seem menacing enough, other combinations are at hand: the "good homosexual," the "good Sandinista," the "good feminist," the "good labor union leader," the "good capitalist"—simply pick the combination most calculated to offend whoever is being addressed, and that will re-create the anger Jesus' hearers must have experienced after his own verbal twist.

When we ask for a definition of the neighbor, along the lines of the lawyer's query, the story gives us a pretty clear answer. The neighbor is not just a close friend or someone belonging to our part of society; the neighbor is *anyone in need*. It is an example of Jesus' skill as a storyteller that he never identifies the man by the side of the road; he is only "a man," which means anyone at all (male or female, we had better add, since the biblical word doesn't convey that clearly), lacking identification, Social Security number, and three notarized references of good character for use in applying for jobs or welfare. In the United States, an "undocumented worker" is about as close as we can come to "a man (or woman)." To us, an undocumented worker is someone without a name, without a number (which is even worse), who probably doesn't even have a legal right to be here. If the "someone" is from, let us say, El Salvador, she may have fled because her government's hit squads were trying to murder her for speaking out against governmental repression. But this only makes her need for anonymity greater, for if the United States Immigration Service tracks her down and gets hold of her, it will probably follow its clearly defined policy and ship her back to El Salvador on the first available flight, where she is likely to be shot. So much for neighborliness in high places.

On this reading of the story, then, the neighbor is anyone I meet along the way, or even, as Gustavo Gutiérrez says, commenting on this reading of the parable, "the one who comes to me for help," to whom I am to give aid and assistance.

Now to have arrived at such a conclusion is a considerable ethical achievement, and the story has encouraged people to act with compassion for two millennia. But, as Gutiérrez and others from the third world remind us, *the story tells us more than this.* For if this represents our full understanding of neighborliness, then there is *no need for change* in our world; it can remain basically the same. Such a view of neighborliness does not call us to move beyond our accustomed routines; it is only those along our way whom we need to view as neighbors. Gutiérrez presses the point, almost harshly: "All social reformism is a 'love' that stays on its own front porch" (*The Power of the Poor in History,* p. 44).

2. So let us return to Jesus' exchange with the lawyer. As we have seen, in response to the lawyer's abstract question, Jesus tells a story, after which he returns a question to the lawyer. But *it is an entirely different question:* "Which of these three," he asks, referring to the priest, the Levite, and the Samaritan, "do you think *proved neighbor* to the man who fell among the robbers?" (Luke 10:36, italics added). The lawyer's question was abstract and definitional; Jesus' question is specific and action-oriented. So in terms of Jesus' question, it is not the person by the side of the road who defines neighborliness for us, but the

good Samaritan who enacts it. The neighbor is the Samaritan rather than the one in need.

Ernesto Cardenal and the community at Solentiname reached this same conclusion when the Lukan passage was their Gospel lesson at Mass. It wasn't easy. Cardenal first reminded his friends:

> "We're accustomed to thinking that this parable is to make us see that the Samaritan is the one who loved his neighbor, and what Jesus asks at the end of the parable is which of the three who passed by on the road *was the neighbor* of the wounded man."
>
> One answered: "The man without religion was the neighbor."
>
> "It wasn't the wounded man?" [an earlier impression, dying hard]
>
> "It wasn't the wounded man." . . .
>
> Felipe: "It seems that instead it's the one who serves that's the neighbor."
>
> (*The Gospel in Solentiname,* Vol. 3, p. 98)

Gutiérrez offers the same conclusion: The neighbor was not the wounded man, "the neighbor was the Samaritan who *approached* the wounded man and *made him his neighbor*" (*A Theology of Liberation,* p. 198).

How does the Samaritan embody being a neighbor? First, he *approaches* the wounded man. He enters into the wounded man's situation. And it may be important to the discussion that it is a "wounded" man who is the recipient of the Samaritan's concern. Some of us might choose to "approach" only those like ourselves, or those not seriously disadvantaged by society. José Miranda suggests the importance of some priorities in this matter and is characteristically willing to be specific. The story is concerned, he says, about "not just any man but *a man who had suffered injustice and violence* and needed help from someone who was able to have com-passion on him" (Miranda, *Communism in the Bible,* p. 63, italics added).

The word "compassion," which is important in Miranda's text, helps us understand the quality of the "approach," for it is important in the biblical text as well. To have compassion, etymologically, means "to suffer with." It means to suffer alongside, to enter fully into the situation of the other, sharing whatever comes. The initiative is not taken to fulfill some formal religious obligation but to act out of care and concern for the other. The Greek word referring to "compassion" in verse 32, Gutiérrez notes, can be translated, "because his heart was melting." But this does not mean sheer individual concern; for, as Miranda establishes after lengthy exegetical examination, "compassion" really means "interhuman justice."

The second thing Gutiérrez highlights is that by approaching the wounded man, the Samaritan *made him his neighbor. Being* a neighbor makes the one who is approached into a neighbor also. In this sense, Gutiérrez can affirm, "The neighbor is not [the one] whom I find in my path but rather [the one] in whose path I place myself, [the one] whom I approach and actively seek" (Gutiérrez, *The Power of the Poor in History,* p. 198).

There is no tidy fence around the area in which I must "actively seek" the one who now becomes a neighbor. The neighbor is the one *from afar* whom I approach, "the one for whom I must search," as Gutiérrez puts it, "everywhere"—in factories, slums, farms, mines.

The head trip (abstract definition) has become a foot trip (active seeking).

When this begins to happen, the world *will* change, along with our ways of acting with it. All those things that create barriers between neighbors, thus understood, must be challenged, smashed if necessary, and rebuilt.

Back once more to Jesus and the lawyer, who for quite a while now has been developing a case of sweaty palms. Jesus, having told his story in such a way as to wipe out the appropriateness of the lawyer's question, has offered a counterquestion: "Which of these three, do you think, *proved neighbor* to the man who fell among the robbers?"

Pity the plight of the lawyer: he who sought to entrap Jesus in the beginning is entrapped by Jesus in the end. What can he possibly reply to Jesus' question except "The one who showed mercy on him"? He must have known, with a sinking feeling, that the circle of entrapment was complete. For what can Jesus possibly reply to him except "Go and act the same way yourself" (Luke 10:37, slightly paraphrased)? The head trip has been demolished, the foot trip has begun.

It is not wise to tangle with Jesus, even if you have a Ph.D.

OTHER BIBLICAL PASSAGES

Here we face an embarrassment of riches, for "love of neighbor" is a pervasive biblical theme.

The first letter of John is particularly good on the relationship between love of God and love of neighbor, and a number of excerpts from it are cited in Chapter 9. The comment of the Johannine writer, "Love must not be a matter of words or talk; it must be genuine and show itself in action" (1 John 3:18), summarizes the shift in the Lukan passage from head trip to foot trip. The same emphasis emerges in Jesus' vision of the Last Judgment, the subject of Chapter 9.

To confront the demands love makes, it is almost enough to concentrate on 1 Corinthians 13, although this passage (like the present one) suffers from overfamiliarity. The notion, however, that actions performed without love are empty and meaningless (like noisy gongs or clanging cymbals) is unpalatable and therefore challenging, when removed from the bathos that surrounds so much of our reading of Paul's "hymn to love."

To flesh out references to the Samaritan's quality of "compassion," a study of the book of Hosea is instructive, and the interrelationship of love, justice, grace, and righteousness in the

Bible is well developed in Miranda, *Marx and the Bible,* especially chapter 2.

ITEMS FOR REFLECTION AND DISCUSSION

1. Ernesto Cardenal's troublesome fisherfolk keep intruding into our tidy middle-class universe. Laureano, recalling that the Samaritan had no religion and was being set up in opposition to professional religious types, draws a conclusion about our world:

> "The people" are the wounded man who's bleeding to death on the highway. The religious folk, who are not impressed by the people's problems, are those two that were going to the temple to pray. The atheists, who are the revolutionaries, are the Good Samaritan of the parable, the good companion, the good comrade.
>
> *(The Gospel in Solentiname,* Vol. 3, p. 99, slightly altered)

Is Laureano describing a world we know anything about?

2. What do Jesus' question and the lawyer's answer suggest about being "neighbors" today, in relation to *(a)* legislation to protect the rights of minority groups, *(b)* the diminution of social services for the poor, and *(c)* the United States' manipulation of the destinies of small nations in Central America?

3. What would "active seeking" for the neighbor mean in the life of the church? Consider Gutiérrez' insistence that this is what lies behind the Latin American church's decision to make a "preferential option for the poor." Where are the poor, he asks, for whom the church makes this option? Certainly not in church. Certainly not in the parts of town where people of the better class live. The poor dwell in the *barrios,* the slums; they are tenant farmers trying to scratch a living out of the wretched pieces of land the wealthy *patrón* rents to them at exorbitant rates; they are in the mines where the wages are

indecent and anyone who tries to organize the workers gets fired; they are in the prisons being tortured to reveal who gave them subversive ideas about the right to adequate shelter and medical care. To make a "'preferential option" for such people is to leave the safe world of head trips, engage in foot trips to such places, and help the oppressed organize to challenge the oppressors.

What would be North American analogues to this kind of commitment?

4. An exercise in imagination:

We enter the world of the parable. We, too, go down from Jerusalem to Jericho. We encounter a woman who fell among thieves and, by grace, do not pass by on the other side but treat her with compassion. The next week we repeat the trip and encounter a similar victim whom we likewise treat with compassion. Twice during the following month we have to make the trip (business is brisk just before the holiday season), and each time there is another victim to be treated.

By now a thought has occurred to us: "This is a stupid way to respond. We keep binding up victims every time we make the trip, but nothing changes. Binding up wounds isn't enough; we've got to ensure that people don't need to be bound up in the first place."

So next week at the town council the local alderman, responding to our phone calls, introduces preventive legislation: (1) nobody can make the trip alone, unless he or she is adequately armed and able to ward off attack; (2) the number of patrol cars on the road will be doubled as a message to potential brigands; and (3) no nighttime travel will be allowed until we pass a local bond issue to get better lighting, especially at the hairpin curve where four out of every five robberies occur.

Such measures may make the road a little safer and virtually eliminate highway robberies and muggings, though the tax rate will soar. But the thieves, who are not stupid, will simply transfer their activities to areas more conducive to their personal health and longevity, and there will be a sudden rash of house-breakings in suburban Jericho.

More radical steps are necessary ("radical" in the sense of getting to the *radix,* or root, of the trouble). Those who want to meet the problem will have to ask such questions as: Why do so many people steal in the first place? Is it because they can't get jobs? (There is a high correlation between upward rates of unemployment and upward rates of crime.) Do we provide so little good education for young people that they turn to beating up travelers out of frustration or boredom? Are the thieves facing debts they can't pay off because interest rates are exorbitant? What percentage of the thieves are from minority groups —the last hired and the first fired—who thus have lots of time for moonlighting? Whose job is it to deal with these problems?

8. TRANSFIGURATION: ECSTASY AND EPILEPSY
(Changing Location)

Luke 9:28–43

There have been attempts throughout Christian history to separate worship and action, prayer and politics. Recently the charge has been made against third world "liberation theology," for example, that it reduces the gospel to "mere politics" or is guilty of "horizontalism," an ethical perspective devoid of a "vertical" relationship to God. We have already seen how wide of the mark such charges are.

There has been a new twist to our domestic discussion of such issues. Those who once declared most vehemently that "religion and politics don't mix" have now decided that the issue is no longer "politics" but only a certain kind of politics, namely, "left-wing politics." Right-wing politics are O.K. So it is commonplace now for TV evangelists and sophisticated conservatives to support bigger defense budgets, capital punishment, and any measures, nuclear war included, designed to "fight communism"—all in the name of Christ.

At least the lines of the battle have been redrawn. We no longer need to ask, "Do religion and politics mix?" since the answer is, "Of course they do." Instead, we need to examine the nature of the mix.

Our task in this chapter is to consider biblical resources that help us keep the two sides of life—worship and action—in constant interplay, in order to *establish as great a degree of congruence as we can between the nature of the God we worship and the nature of the human actions we undertake in God's name.* Christians who support bigger and bigger defense budgets, for example, need to wrestle with the incongruity between that position and the God whom they worship whenever they recite Psalm 46, which declares, "From end to end of the earth [God] stamps out war: [God] breaks the bow, [God] snaps the spear and burns the shield in the fire" (Ps. 46:8–9, NEB). God's clear intent here is to destroy old weapons rather than build new ones. And it will not do to reply that the Pentagon budget is not very big on bows and spears and shields, for the contemporary counterpart of a "bow" would be an M1 rifle, the counterpart of a "spear" would be a Trident missile capable of destroying sixty-four cities, while the counterpart of a "shield" might be a policy of nuclear deterrence.

This is only a single example of the need to keep exploring the nature of the mix between our so-called "religious" and our so-called "secular" activity and to find ways in which liturgy and lobbying, prayer and politics, devotions and democracy, songs and social engagement, Bibles and ballots, can be seen as two sides of the same coin.

There are two episodes (or so they are usually interpreted) in Jesus' ministry that can focus our discussion. The point will be to suggest that they are not two episodes but one.

THE BIBLICAL TEXT: LUKE 9:28–43

[28]Now about eight days after these sayings he took with him Peter and John and James, and went up on the mountain to pray. [29]And as he was praying, the appearance of his countenance was altered, and his raiment became dazzling white. [30]And behold, two men talked with him, Moses and Elijah, [31]who appeared in glory and spoke of his departure, which he was to accomplish at Jerusalem. [32]Now Peter and those who were with him were heavy with sleep, and when they wakened they saw his glory and

the two men who stood with him. [33]And as the men were parting from him, Peter said to Jesus, "Master, it is well that we are here; let us make three booths, one for you and one for Moses and one for Elijah"—not knowing what he said. [34]As he said this, a cloud came and overshadowed them; and they were afraid as they entered the cloud. [35]And a voice came out of the cloud, saying, "This is my Son, my Chosen; listen to him!" [36]And when the voice had spoken, Jesus was found alone. And they kept silence and told no one in those days anything of what they had seen.

[37]On the next day, when they had come down from the mountain, a great crowd met him. [38]And behold, a man from the crowd cried, "Master, I beg you to look upon my son, for he is my only child; [39]and behold, a spirit seizes him, and he suddenly cries out; it convulses him till he foams, and shatters him, and will hardly leave him. [40]And I begged your disciples to cast it out, but they could not." [41]Jesus answered, "O faithless and perverse generation, how long am I to be with you and bear with you? Bring your son here." [42]While he was coming, the demon tore him and convulsed him. But Jesus rebuked the unclean spirit, and healed the boy, and gave him back to his father. [43]And all were astonished at the majesty of God.

It's been a rugged time, the past week or so. Jesus and his followers have been up north, taking stock. The kingdom isn't exactly appearing overnight. But there has been a moment of clarification. Jesus has asked the disciples who people say that he is, and he has gotten the usual responses: John the Baptist, Elijah, one of the prophets. But then he asks the harder question, "Who do *you* say that I am?" (Luke 9:20, italics added), and Peter answers, "The Christ of God" ("Christos" being the Greek equivalent of the Hebrew word "Messiah," which means God's "Anointed One")—even though in Matthew's parallel account it is immediately clear that Peter is operating in totally characteristic fashion: he hasn't the foggiest notion of what he's talking about.

All twelve disciples must be having second thoughts. For Jesus seizes the moment to spell out some implications of Peter's confession that have not occurred to Peter. Mincing no words, he tells them that to be "the Christ of God" will mean getting murdered, probably within a fortnight.

As if that isn't enough of a downer, he tells them that what is in store for the Messiah is in store for the Messiah's followers as well: "If there are those who would come after me, let them deny themselves and take up their crosses daily and follow me" (Luke 9:24, adapted). (The word "crosses," we may be sure, was no euphemism to Jesus' listeners, who had never seen crosses dangling over the stomachs of princes of the church but had seen plenty of crosses used as instruments of torture and very, very slow death.)

And then, just to take it out of the realm of talk, Jesus starts walking—swiftly—toward Jerusalem, which just happens to be the headquarters of the strongest opposition to the whole crowd of disciples, a city where getting strung up on crosses, if not exactly a way of life, is uniformly a way of death.

So it's been a rugged time, and now, after eight days on the road, Jesus takes Peter, John, and James up a nearby mountain to share in a bit of stiff praying and get their spiritual houses in order for the heavy going they will have in Jerusalem.

What begins as a regular prayer session rapidly escalates into a vision. Jesus' appearance changes and his followers see him in conversation with Moses and Elijah. To third world readers, the presence of these particular figures is significant, for Moses is the great liberator who led Israel out of the clutches of Pharaoh, and Elijah is the prophet "who defended the poor and oppressed," as Ernesto Cardenal describes him. Since their discussion appears to have been about the coming showdown in Jerusalem, concern for the poor and oppressed who need liberation seems likely to have had top billing.

How do Peter, John, and James react? There is more intensity on the mountaintop than they can cope with, and in a preview of their performance a few days later in a Jerusalem garden, they respond by almost falling asleep. (Let us acknowledge that eight grueling days on the road may also have taken their toll.) When they get past their grogginess, the atmosphere is even more charged: they see the "glory" (vs. 31, 32). "Glory" is a special biblical word denoting the awesome sense of God's presence. And as the vision begins to fade, Peter, who was never one to think before speaking, blurts out, "Let's make three booths," recalling the Feast of Booths commemorating the giving of the Law. "Let's stay up here," he seems to be saying. "Let's build a retreat center, complete with meditation chapels, and hang on to this 'religious experience' so that it won't fade away." This would be a particularly attractive suggestion, since crosses in Jerusalem have recently been presented as the only alternative.

His motion, however, dies for want of a second, as the sense of mystery increases. The disciples are both *(a)* afraid and *(b)* silent as a cloud envelops them; these are not bad responses to the awesome. A voice out of the cloud affirms Jesus (much as a similar voice—or the same voice—had affirmed him at his baptism), "This is my Son, my Chosen; listen to him!"

And then it's all over and the three are alone with Jesus. Even Peter maintains silence, which is about as impressive testimony as one could imagine for the overwhelming nature of the experience. The next morning, when they go back down the mountain (leaving no booths), they are still too overwhelmed to talk about it.

How does Jesus react? While it seems presumptuous to put ourselves in Jesus' shoes, we can pick up a few clues from the narrative.

Jesus knows better than anyone else what lies in store for them when they get to Jerusalem. So when he breaks the trip to go apart to pray, he clearly feels an intense need to do some retooling before the tough times start.

Whatever he may have hoped for in going up the mountain, he gets even more. First, he receives a strong sense of being in continuity with God's ongoing work, for there could scarcely be a better succession to follow than Moses and Elijah. And second, the voice from the cloud communicates assurance that what he has been about since his baptism is on target.

Jesus does not respond to Peter's suggestion that they stay on the mountaintop and keep the ecstasy alive. In Chapter 1 we discovered that Jesus left Emmaus the moment the "religious experience" was over, since the action was no longer in Emmaus; here we discover that the action is no longer on the mountaintop.

Where *is* the action? Down at the bottom of the mountain. Jesus' descent leads *immediately* into a response to human need, the healing of an epileptic boy (vs. 37–43).

A number of themes are treated in this part of the overall episode, but what is important for us is the *fact* that the overall episode ends here and not on the mountaintop. For when the distraught father of the epileptic boy asks for help, Jesus does not respond, "Look, I've just had a marvelous experience and I don't want to lose the glow. Have the disciples check out the boy. Luke's a doctor, and if it's something he can't handle perhaps I can give you an appointment next Tuesday at nine." No, things are immediately earthy, human, even ugly—for a person in the midst of an epileptic seizure is not a pretty sight.

It is all of a piece—ecstasy and epilepsy. *This* is what Messiahship is all about: being in the midst of the poor, the sick, the helpless, those with frothing mouths. Messiahship—like Christian living—is not just "mountaintop experiences" or "acts of concern for human welfare"; it is *a necessary combination of the two.*

OTHER BIBLICAL PASSAGES

To juxtapose a story of religious exaltation and a story of human need, and to claim that they are *one* story, might seem like special pleading. But this pattern of interrelationship is constantly repeated in the Bible. Let us recall some of the passages considered in this book.

The Emmaus story centers on "the breaking of the bread," the central experience of worship for Christians. Jesus' liturgical act not only clarifies what has been happening but also sends the disciples back to Jerusalem on their way to the ends of the earth. The worship leads to the action.

The exodus story. The Israelites want a three-day pass in order to go into the wilderness to worship God. Yahweh's famous liberation cry, "Let my people go," continues, "that they may hold a feast to me in the wilderness" (Ex. 5:1). This intensely *political* event, challenging the power of the Pharaoh, soon becomes the most intensely *liturgical* event in Judaism— the Passover. The central event of Christian spirituality, the Eucharist, is an adaptation of the Passover meal, so it too grows out of a political event.

The encounter between Jeremiah and Jehoiakim portrays the fusion of politics and devotion, for, as we saw, it is likely that the description of Josiah as one who "ate and drank" and "did justice and righteousness" (Jer. 22:15) refers to his sharing in the covenant meal with Yahweh, an act of worship that is directly linked to the doing of justice.

There is a further connection between Jeremiah 22 and Christian worship, with Jeremiah 31 providing the link. Jeremiah 22, we recall, emphasizes that "to know God is to do justice." Then in Jeremiah 31 there is the famous announcement of the "new covenant," the chief characteristic of which will be that "they shall all *know me,* from the least of them to the greatest, says the Lord" (Jer. 31:34, italics added). To "know God," in Jeremiah 31, has the same meaning as to "know God" in Jeremiah 22; both refer to the doing of justice. And it is from the new covenant passages in Jeremiah that Jesus quotes in the upper room when he initiates the Lord's Supper: "This cup," he says, "is the *new covenant* in my blood" (Luke 22:20, italics added; cf. also Matt. 26:28; Mark 14:24; 1 Cor. 11:23–25). So Jesus' inauguration of the "new covenant" is his inauguration of a new era of justice, and the Lord's Supper is the Christian celebration of that fact.

Tissa Balasuriya, a Sri Lankan priest, has taken great pains to remind us of this. In *The Eucharist and Human Liberation* he emphasizes that the central act of Christian worship is the celebration of a *political* act of liberation by God, and that every repetition of the Eucharist should signify a new commitment to the struggle for justice. Fr. Balasuriya chides us for having tamed the Eucharist, distorting its revolutionary implications into a time for reaffirming the status quo. But he takes heart from the fact that as the true roots of the original event are being rediscovered in the third world, the dynamic for change is returning. True celebration of the Eucharist is an act of revolutionary politics. Any smart dictator will forbid it on pain of death.

The Magnificat. If we were to read the latter portion of Mary's song and did not know its source, we would assume that it had been delivered—probably rather stridently—at a left-wing political rally called to initiate a march on the Capitol, if not the White House. Where else would we hear about overthrowing the mighty from their seats of power and raising up the poor to take their place, or giving food to the hungry and stripping the rich of their possessions? The unexpected answer is that we would hear it in the prayer of a young Jewish girl making her act of devotion to God. No one who reads this passage (or, better still, prays it) can ever again believe that private worship is irrelevant to what we call real life. Mary's song is so close to real life as to scare the living daylights out of people who think they have real life under control.

Jesus' "political" message at Nazareth is not presented at a rally in the fourth precinct, nor is the text he reads drawn from a political tract. The place is worship in the synagogue and the text is Holy Scripture (which is beginning to look like a "political tract" after all). Few events more clearly illustrate the interrelationship of piety and politics than that charged service in

Nazareth, when a time of worship became a launching pad for a program so radical that the hearers wanted to break the speaker's neck.

The story of the good Samaritan. Here the characters who come off worst are the religious "professionals," whose job is to look after prayer and worship in the Temple; they fail to make a connection between what they do in the Temple and what they are doing on the road. No increase in pious prayers, lighting of candles, or recitation of Hail Marys can obliterate the glaring fact that someone is in need and they are ignoring him.

The story of the fiery furnace (Daniel 3:1–18). In this passage, yet to be examined, it is the worshiping habits of three young Jews that get them into political trouble. They refuse to worship any god but the God of Israel. This greatly annoys the king, who has just decreed that everybody, without exception, must worship a golden image. And the Jews, by the "religious" act of obeying God, simultaneously engage in the "political" act of disobeying the king—a "political" act that is derived from, and is absolutely consistent with, its "religious" roots.

ITEMS FOR REFLECTION AND DISCUSSION

1. Discuss Charles Péguy's statement "Everything begins in mysticism and ends in politics." Does this fit the transfiguration story? Have you ever observed examples of its truth? Would the reverse sequence hold?

2. Are there examples (either good or bad) out of our own culture in which the life of worship has contributed to the political insights and activities of the worshipers? Would the reverse sequence hold here too?

3. In the Eastern church calendar, August 6 is the Feast of the Transfiguration, celebrating the event described in our text. In the Western secular calendar, August 6 is the anniversary of the dropping of the first atomic bomb on Hiroshima. Each anniversary exemplifies a certain kind of power that brought

about a certain kind of "transfiguration" that changed the course of history. What are the characteristics of these different kinds of power? What odds would you give if they were pitted directly against each other?

4. In the Latin American church, a great deal of attention is given to what is called a *praxis* model of social change, "praxis" being defined as the ongoing interrelation between reflection and action: we act, then we reflect on our action; that reflection enables us to act more effectively, which in turn enables us to reflect more creatively, so that we can then act more effectively —and so on. (See the fuller discussion in Chapter 1.) Can you see this working in events surrounding the transfiguration episode? Possible model: action (feeding the five thousand), reflection ("Who do you say that I am?"), action ("We are going up to Jerusalem,"), reflection (going up the Mount of Transfiguration), action (coming down the mountain and healing the epileptic boy), and so on. What would this suggest about the relationship of worship and action in our own situations?

5. How much do you identify with Peter, John, and James in wanting to stay up on the mountain, safe from crosses and children with foaming mouths? There is a hymn that describes their struggle. See to what extent it describes your own. The early verses extol life on top of the mountain, each verse repeating the refrain, "How good, Lord, to be here!"—enumerating all the spiritual pluses that would accrue if only they could "make this hill our home." But they finally agree to change location, and the last lines read:

> How good, Lord, to be here!
> Yet we may not remain;
> But, since you bid us leave the mount,
> Come with us to the plain.
> > ("How Good, Lord, to Be Here!" by Joseph Armitage
> > Robinson; *The Australian Hymnal,* 390)

9. JESUS' VISION:
A TASK FOR THE NATIONS
(Changing the Answer)

Matthew 25:31–46

All of us would like the world to be a better place. We may
not agree on just how bad it is or exactly what remedies are
appropriate, but we know that many people get a raw deal, that
it's not always their fault, and that things should be different.

Many individual Christians try to make things different. Albert Schweitzer left a brilliant career in Europe as a philosopher
and musician to become a doctor in Africa; Mother Teresa
joined a religious order and works among the plague-ridden and
dying of Calcutta. Such lives demonstrate individual response to
the needs of the sick, the hungry, the naked—acts of compassion
on which Jesus puts a high premium, as we will shortly discover.

The question posed to us by third world Christians, however,
is whether individual attention to massive social ills, admirable
as it is, is sufficient. They tell us—on the basis of the text we are
about to study—that it is not.

THE BIBLICAL TEXT: MATTHEW 25:31–46

[31]"When the Son of man comes in his glory, and all
the angels with him, then he will sit on his glorious throne.
[32]Before him will be gathered all the nations, and he will
separate them one from another as a shepherd separates
the sheep from the goats, [33]and he will place the sheep at
his right hand, but the goats at the left. [34]Then the King

will say to those at his right hand, 'Come, O blessed of my
Father, inherit the kingdom prepared for you from the
foundation of the world; [35]for I was hungry and you gave
me food, I was thirsty and you gave me drink, I was a
stranger and you welcomed me, [36]I was naked and you
clothed me, I was sick and you visited me, I was in prison
and you came to me.' [37]Then the righteous will answer
him, 'Lord, when did we see thee hungry and feed thee,
or thirsty and give thee drink? [38]And when did we see thee
a stranger and welcome thee, or naked and clothe thee?
[39]And when did we see thee sick or in prison and visit
thee?' [40]And the King will answer them, 'Truly, I say to
you, as you did it to one of the least of these my brethren,
you did it to me.' [41]Then he will say to those at his left
hand, 'Depart from me, you cursed, into the eternal fire
prepared for the devil and his angels; [42]for I was hungry
and you gave me no food, I was thirsty and you gave me
no drink, [43]I was a stranger and you did not welcome me,
naked and you did not clothe me, sick and in prison and
you did not visit me.' [44]Then they also will answer, 'Lord,
when did we see thee hungry or thirsty or a stranger or
naked or sick or in prison, and did not minister to thee?'
[45]Then he will answer them, 'Truly, I say to you, as you
did it not to one of the least of these, you did it not to me.'
[46]And they will go away into eternal punishment, but the
righteous into eternal life."

We previously examined a story of Jesus in which he *changes
the question* that has been directed at him. In this passage we
examine a vision of Jesus in which he *changes the answer* from
the one to which we have been accustomed.

He does so by sharing his version of the Last Judgment. One
wing of Christianity has compressed the entire Christian message into a single vivid and terrifying tableau: Most people
(usually those who haven't "accepted Jesus Christ as their personal Lord and Savior" or may say they have but haven't *really*)
will be damned eternally. A few (usually the self-appointed

clerical scorekeepers) will be saved. The motivation for living well is fear.

It is curious that the Christians who most confidently offer this scenario claim to be biblically minded, even though the Bible devotes little space to their version of the theme. As José Miranda points out, the text before us is "the only detailed description which the New Testament gives us of a last judgment" (Miranda, *Marx and the Bible,* p. 19). It is even more curious that its "detailed description" bears scarcely any resemblance to conventional Last Judgment scenarios.

We need, therefore, to discard most of the theological baggage that has been imposed on this passage and try to hear it afresh. It does not offer a blueprint for a datable future event which some clairvoyant reporter has provided in advance. Nor is it really a parable, though it is often so called. A parable begins with something familiar—a woman losing a coin, a boy running away from home, a man falling among thieves—and uses it as a pointer to the unfamiliar, such as some quality of the kingdom of God that would never have occurred to us unaided. In this text we have at best a parable-in-reverse, for it moves from the *un*familiar (the presence of angels, a cosmic tribunal) to the familiar (visiting a prisoner, providing food for a hungry person), with sheep and goats as the connecting link.

It will be more useful, therefore, to consider the text as a vision, a picture painted on a large canvas, trying to communicate *pictorially* (by images) what cannot be communicated *linguistically* (by words).

Matthew mounts the picture on an easel toward the conclusion of his Gospel. Jesus has gotten to Jerusalem, and the anticipated showdown (which we indicated in the last chapter) has developed with the religious and political authorities, who want him off the scene—permanently. In just a few days he has tangled with them over the dilemma of giving allegiance to both God and Caesar; lashed out harshly against the Pharisees ("hypocrites . . . serpents . . . brood of vipers"); mourned with

tender solicitude over the fate of Jerusalem; spoken of signs of
the approaching "end," displaying a degree of modesty about
predicting its time of arrival that many of his followers have
failed to emulate; and told a batch of parables. Jesus' days are
numbered and he knows it, so there is an urgency to everything
he says and does. This is the context in which his vision of the
Last Judgment is unveiled.

The Son of Man (a title for Jesus himself) is holding court.
A separation among those standing before him takes place, like
the separation a shepherd makes between his sheep and his goats
when they are brought in from the field. The categories are
value-laden to the nth degree: the "sheep" are commended, the
"goats" condemned.

The sheep—the righteous—are told that they will enter the
kingdom of heaven, for they responded to human need:

> I was hungry and you gave me food,
> I was thirsty and you gave me drink,
> I was a stranger and you welcomed me,
> I was naked and you clothed me,
> I was sick and you visited me,
> I was in prison and you came to me.
>   (Matt. 25:35–36; cf. 37–39, 42–43, 44)

Although this is splendid news, the sheep, instead of being
elated, are bewildered. There must have been a mistake. Much
as they would like to take credit for having done such things for
Jesus, they really can't. "When," they ask, "did we see *you*
hungry and feed *you,* or thirsty and give *you* drink?"—and so
on, through a litany that Matthew reproduces a second time.
Jesus responds, "Truly, I say to you, as you did it to one of the
least of these my brethren, you did it to me."

That would be a pleasant, upbeat way to conclude: a story
with a happy ending, a painting with strong positive colors, by
which to proclaim the good news that the sheep have made it.

But the story has a flip side; the painting has a somber cast.

There are also the goats, and the goats don't make it. Stylistically and substantively, their half of the text is a mirror image of the first half. They will *not* enter the kingdom of heaven, for they have *not* responded to human need: "I was hungry and you gave me *no* food, I was thirsty and you gave me *no* drink," and so on, through the litany for a third time.

The goats are bewildered too, which is the one thing they share in common with the sheep. There must have been a mistake. When did they ever see Jesus hungry and *not* feed him, naked and *not* clothe him—and so on, through the litany for a fourth and final time. They receive the same reply the sheep received, save that in their case it is in the negative: "Truly, I say to you, as you did it *not* to one of the least of these, you did it *not* to me" (Matt. 25:45).

The vision has a definitive two-line conclusion, continuing in a gloomy mood save for the grace note of hope at the very end: "And [the unrighteous] will go away into eternal punishment, but the righteous into eternal life" (Matt. 25:46).

OTHER BIBLICAL PASSAGES

The First Letter of John provides a bonanza of supporting materials for our passage. Its relatively late time of composition demonstrates that the themes in Jesus' vision are not discarded by his followers as too idealistic or impractical but continue to be affirmed. A sampling:

> If we say, "We love God," while hating our sisters and brothers, we are liars. If we do not love the sisters or brothers whom we have seen, it cannot be said that we love God whom we have not seen. (1 John 4:20, adapted)

> But if we have enough to live on, and yet when we see our sisters and brothers in need shut up our hearts against them, how can it be said that the divine love dwells in us? My children, love must not be a matter of words or talk;

it must be genuine and show itself in action. (1 John
3:17–18, adapted)

The Letter of James (which some Christians have looked
upon as second rate because Luther described it as "an epistle
of straw" and wished that it had been omitted from the canon)
is further corroboration of the themes of Matthew 25:31–46.
The fact that James is widely used in third world churches today
suggests that the wisdom of those who created the canon may
have been a cut above Luther's. A key notion in James is that
"faith apart from works is barren" (James 2:20). Some of
James's words are an almost perfect commentary on the words
of the Son of Man in Matthew 25:

> What does it profit, sisters and brothers, if we say that we
> have faith but have not works? Can our faith save us? If
> a sister or brother is ill-clad and in lack of daily food, and
> one of us says to them, "Go in peace, be warmed and
> filled," without giving them the things needed for the
> body, what does it profit? So faith, by itself, if it has no
> works, is dead. (James 2:14–17, adapted)

ITEMS FOR REFLECTION AND DISCUSSION

Let us first review some of the insights that Christians in our
own culture have found in this passage.

1. The vision reminds us that *we are accountable,* that our
actions have consequences. We cannot take refuge in a theology
that says, "Not to worry. If you haven't done enough, God will
forgive you and Christ has already atoned for your sins." Die-
trich Bonhoeffer rightly called such a view "cheap grace."

2. *What really counts before God is not what we thought.* The
important things are not *(a)* regular church attendance, *(b)*
praying daily, *(c)* knowing the Apostles' Creed, *(d)* tithing, or
even *(e)* confessing Jesus Christ as Lord and Savior. Admirable

though such characteristics of Christian living may be, they do not even rate a passing nod in Jesus' assessment. All that counts in Jesus' assessment is—helping those in need. In case that is not clear on first reading, a handy checklist is included, offering specific suggestions about what helping those in need involves, a list that is repeated *four times* (with only minor variations) in case the misunderstanding should persist.

3. *We love God by serving God's people.* When we support the poor we are not only supporting the poor, we are glorifying God; when we reject the poor we are not only rejecting the poor, we are rejecting God. Jesus makes the same point when he notes that the second commandment (loving the neighbor) is exactly the same as the first (loving God). Paul was even more blunt: "For the whole law is fulfilled in one word, 'You shall love your neighbor as yourself' " (Gal. 5:14).

4. *The "righteous" do not claim to be righteous.* They are surprised to learn that they had been loving God by feeding the poor. "When did *we* see *you* hungry?" they ask the judge. (The unrighteous, also caught off guard, respond in indignation, "When did we see you hungry and not feed you? The very idea!")

Here is where grace comes into play. Salvation is not for those who have toted up their good works ("We did *this* for God today, and *that* for God yesterday, and we can *really* rack up some points over the weekend"). It is a gift given for things done without thought of reward, expressing concern for the neighbor quite apart from knowing that concern for the neighbor is simultaneously concern for God. No wonder the "righteous" are surprised. Those who claim to be the righteous are precisely those to whom the designation will be denied.

5. *The judge who directs attention to the poor and outcast is numbered among the poor and outcast.* The judge is not an abstract or aloof—or terrifying—deity. Rather, the judge is Christ himself, one whose own life was actively identified with

the poor and outcast, which is the surest possible sign we could have that love for God (represented by such a one) and love for the poor (represented by such a one) are inseparable.

All well and good, our third world friends might say, but there is more to it than that. They press us in at least three ways:

1. The words we usually translate "righteous" and "unrighteous" (words without much social clout) are often translated by third world Christians as *"just"* and *"unjust"* (words with terrific social clout). One important aspect of justice, José Miranda reminds us, involves the restoration of what has been stolen. Giving food to the hungry or clothing to the naked is not a charitable handout but an exercise in simple justice—restoring to the poor what is rightfully theirs, what has been taken from them unjustly. So Jesus' vision is not a plea for tax-deductible donations but a fervent cry for justice, for setting right what has gone wrong. The lines are pretty clear, as Ernesto Cardenal suggests during Mass at Solentiname:

> Those who are saved [Jesus] twice calls "the just." In the Bible the "unjust" are those who rob orphans and widows, those who are responsible for there being poor, who get rich at the expense of others, take away lands, commit fraud, are bloody and cruel; in short, they are the oppressors. The "just" are the opposite of all that.
>
> (*The Gospel in Solentiname,* Vol. 4, p. 59)

2. Pressing the argument, Gustavo Gutiérrez insists that "we must *avoid the pitfall of individual charity"* (*A Theology of Liberation,* p. 202), as though the message of Jesus were about one-on-one acts of mercy from and to deserving individuals. When we talk about "the neighbor," we are not just talking about individuals but about a whole network of *social* relationships, exploited social classes, dominated peoples, communities of the oppressed. There is more to relationship than I-Thou.

Alejandro, a worshiper in Solentiname, worries "that the

things Christ names here will be understood as simple traditional charity, and I don't think that's the meaning." Although "traditional charity" may sometimes be all that is possible, Christians need to start thinking about "collectivized charity: a whole system where injustice no longer exists" (Cardenal, p. 51). "Collectivized charity," the worshipers in Solentiname agree, would be the beginning of the kingdom of God.

Handouts to needy individuals are responses to injustice that do not challenge the reasons for injustice. Gutiérrez (p. 202) offers a contrast:

> Charity today is a "political charity." . . . To offer food or drink in our day is a political action; it means the transformation of a society structured to benefit a few who appropriate to themselves the value of the work of others. This transformation ought to be directed toward a radical change in the foundation of society, that is, the private ownership of the means of production.

While North American readers may cringe at the last ten words (and I was tempted to omit them), the logic of the quotation is hard to fault. Since 1980 we have seen that taking social services out of "the public sector" and making them the responsibility of individuals and volunteer groups leaves the poor more dependent than ever on private benevolence. Charity, Gutiérrez insists, involves challenging social structures of injustice and replacing them with structures designed to benefit all people.

3. Gutiérrez is clearly challenging the unspoken assumption that Jesus' vision proposes tests of individual accountability: Did *I* visit the sick? Did *I* provide food for the hungry one outside *my* door? Did *I* enlist in any efforts to help prisoners? And so third world Christians are telling us to look at the text again and ask ourselves, "*Who* are gathered before the Son of Man to be separated from one another?" The answer we usually give, "Individuals whose personal lives are under scrutiny," is simply wrong. *Jesus changes the answer.* Listen: "Before him

will be gathered all *the nations,* and he will separate *them* one from another" (Matt. 25:32, italics added). The vision is not about individual accountability but about corporate accountability. *It is "the nations" that are on trial.*

This is a brand-new ball game, with new rules and a new way of keeping score. If we are going to take our third world friends seriously, we must reexamine Jesus' vision from this new point of view. Let us try.

• *Does our nation feed the hungry and give drink to the thirsty?* Do we see it as the task of our nation to provide resources for the health of the "very least" of our sisters and brothers? Typical example (of which a dozen more could be provided): The budget of the Women, Infants and Children Program (WIC), which provides milk, orange juice, and vitamins for young children of poor working mothers, was slashed almost out of existence at the same time that hundreds of millions of new dollars were budgeted for armaments. Sophisticated weapons systems? Raise the budget. Rudimentary feeding systems? Slash the budget. The awful truth is that nuclear weapons kill even when they are not used, since money goes for them that could otherwise go to alleviating poverty and hunger.

Jesus' vision, moreover, does not define the poor and hungry nationalistically: the "very least" of his sisters and brothers include not only those in Harlem and Appalachia but also those in Calcutta and Concepción. And while it is not the task of our nation to feed all nations, it is the task of every nation to help create structures that provide enough food for all. In our nation today, such a concern is about as far down on the list of governmental priorities as any concern could be. In 1984, in a world of starving children, our administration is paying U.S. farmers millions of dollars *not* to produce milk.

Is this feeding the hungry and giving drink to the thirsty?

• *Does our nation welcome strangers?* The example given in Chapter 7 needs elaboration. In El Salvador, a succession of

U.S.-supported military dictators have systematically murdered civilians who oppose them—over 40,000 in the last four years. In that atmosphere, when Salvadorans know there is a price on their heads, they not unnaturally make their way toward the United States, hoping for asylum as "political refugees," a status to which the United Nations certifies they are legally entitled.

But our Immigration Service (with the backing of the State Department) routinely rounds them up and ships them back to El Salvador to face the likelihood of violent death. The stated reason for the policy is that the fleeing Salvadorans are not really "political refugees"; they have come to the United States only to improve their economic condition. The unstated reason for the policy is that since the United States supports the Salvadoran government, to grant political asylum to Salvadorans—save in the most exceptional cases—would be to acknowledge that the United States is backing a brutal regime. The unstated conclusion can only be that our political image, even if based on deception, is more important than Salvadoran lives. So back go the refugees.

Is this welcoming the strangers?

• *Does our nation clothe the naked?* To clothe the naked today means more than setting up depots in which the cast-off clothing of the rich can be doled out to the poor; it means seeing to it that all people, even and especially "the least," have the minimal necessities of life—clothing, shelter, and (especially) jobs—to enable them to live with enough dignity to buy their own clothes.

Yet since 1980 our national policy has been to cut back on support programs for the poor, asserting that individuals, voluntary groups, or churches should engage in charitable handouts and that "the nation" as a whole does not—contrary to the biblical text—have that responsibility.

Is this clothing the naked?

• *Does our nation visit the sick?* To visit the sick today does not just mean individual hospital calling and bedside prayer, therapeutic as such services may be. It also means "the nation" taking responsibility for adequate facilities for the sick as a right available to all, not as a privilege available only to the affluent. Guillermo, one of the fishermen at Solentiname, got the point: "Christ speaks of visiting the sick; that's the only thing you could do at that time. Now he would have talked of clinics, free medical service, hygienic conditions, preventive medicine" (Cardenal, *The Gospel in Solentiname,* Vol. 4, p. 52).

But health care plans in the United States are available to only a fraction of the population, and their rising cost deprives more and more of the poor of the care they need. Meanwhile the government keeps insisting that its involvement in health care must be diminished.

Is this visiting the sick?

• *Does our nation go to those in prison?* To go to those in prison today does not just mean prison-visitation teams from the Men's Guild every other Thursday. It means concern for the well-being of prisoners, and that means questioning the ability of our prison system to rehabilitate its inmates. Most penologists agree that at least 90 percent of prison inmates should not be there, and that most who emerge from prison have been hardened in the process. To keep the prison system "working," the State of California spends about $14,000 a year per inmate. The mind boggles at what could be done on "the outside" with $14,000 to help an offender learn a trade, get further education, find a job, and become a contributing member of society.

The majority of prisoners are members of minority groups. This is not because they have "criminal mentalities" but because *(a)* they usually come from situations of extreme poverty without the opportunities for good education and gainful employment that are taken for granted in white middle-class suburbs and *(b)* they cannot afford expert legal help once they are in trouble, so that *(c)* they get the harshest sentences. The claim that there are two systems of justice in our country—one for well-to-do whites and one for everybody else—strikes well-to-do whites as a paranoid version of reality, but for everybody else it merely describes what they have experienced.

We have not strayed from the text. Repeat: we have not strayed from the text. The issues we have raised come directly from the text, as we see once we acknowledge that it is "the nations" that stand before the tribunal. But there are at least two more questions.

First question: *Are there nations who are "righteous" according to the vision*—who *do* help those in need and who are *not* aware that they are doing it for Christ?

Surely no nation really meets such criteria, but some nations come closer than others. As an exercise in confronting "unexpected news," let our third world friends offer a candidate. Its name will shock many readers, for it is the object of carefully orchestrated campaigns of vilification by our own government. The name of the nation is Cuba. Even Cuba's severest critics will acknowledge that it qualifies at least on the second score: It is a nation that would express surprise at being told that it was ministering to Jesus or in his name, since (save for a minority of Christians) Cuba's citizens and government would offer humanistic, socialistic, and even communistic reasons, rather than religious ones, for their actions.

But on the first point, Cuba does better when measured by Jesus' checklist than do the Latin American dictatorships that our nation supports. There are national programs to provide enough for those who *hunger and thirst,* so that Cuba's citizens, if not lavishly fed, all get enough; there is a *welcome to strangers,* not only those from third world countries but even those from the United States, who uniformly report that they are treated with respect as individuals rather than categorized as representatives of a hostile government; there is a national commitment to *clothing the naked* by providing jobs for all and by sharing available shelter while new housing is built; there is a strong national commitment to *caring for the sick:* free infirmaries, dispensaries, hospitals, and medical schools are located throughout the island. The record is not as good in relation to *prisons,* for Cuba still has "political prisoners," although its treatment of such prisoners is incomparably better than that accorded in most of the Latin American countries our government supports.

This does not mean that Cuba is a glowing preview of the kingdom of God, or that it is immune from criticism and the need for correction. It does mean that if we take Jesus' vision seriously we are in for some surprises.

Second question: *What about those "goats"?* What about all those nations (our own included?) who descriptively belong in the second category, those who have *not* provided for the hungry and thirsty, who have *not* welcomed the stranger, who have *not* clothed the naked, who have *not* visited the sick, who have *not* gone to those in prison?

At least nobody will be lonesome; there will be a large crowd gathered at the entrance marked "Goats." Perhaps the *urgency* of the vision (recall the hectic circumstances under which Jesus first shared it) is to remind us that it has *not yet* come to pass and there is still time to turn in new directions, so that the actual final accounting can differ from the one Jesus depicts. A direction signal:

The scene: Geneva, 1966, at a conference of the World Council of Churches on "Christians in the Technical and Social Revolutions of Our Time."

The context: The first occasion that third world Christians have had sufficient voice and votes to challenge the unequal distribution of the world's goods.

The speaker: Barbara Ward, a British economist with an unusual sensitivity to such issues.

The comment:

Christians alone straddle the whole spectrum of rich nations, and therefore Christians are a lobby or can be a lobby of incomprehensible importance. . . . And if we don't do it, and we come ultimately before our Heavenly Father, and he says, "Did you feed them, and did you give them to drink, did you clothe them, did you shelter them?" and we say, "Sorry, Lord, but we did give 0.3% of our gross national product," I don't think it will be enough. (Report, *World Conference on Church and Society, Geneva, July 12–26, 1966,* p. 19; Geneva, 1967)

10. FURNACES AND FAITH: "BUT IF NOT . . . "
(Unchanging Allegiance)

Daniel 3:1–18 (selections)

We have been trying to respond to the Bible's insistence on the need for change—changing methods, perspectives, priorities, sides, structures, directions. This could leave the impression that change is the name of the game and that everything is in flux, with today's truths no more than tomorrow's illusions.

In this kind of situation, we long for something unchanging, something secure and stable, on which we can count. In W. H. Auden's Christmas poem "For the Time Being," Joseph, confronted with some unsettling news about a pregnant fiancée, cries out to God, "All I ask is one important and elegant proof . . . that your will is Love." And it is our frequent, if unspoken, wistful hope that the words of the hymn will be answered:

> Change and decay in all around I see;
> O thou who changest not, abide with me.

What we would like, if not "one important and elegant proof," would be some sort of assurance that there is One on whom we can rely and that the allegiance we offer will make a difference. If we could count on God, we could take risks. But if not even God is reliable any more . . .

It is precisely the threat that "not even God is reliable any more" that faces three young Jews living under an ancient dictatorship. The story, in a setting far removed from our own, deals with problems at least as contemporary as this morning's newspaper and tonight's telecast. It undermines expectations like those expressed above and sends us in new directions.

THE BIBLICAL TEXT: DANIEL 3:1–18 (SELECTIONS)

3:1King Nebuchadnezzar made an image of gold, whose height was sixty cubits and its breadth six cubits. He set it up on the plain of Dura, in the province of Babylon. 2Then King Nebuchadnezzar sent to assemble . . . all the officials of the provinces to come to the dedication of the image which King Nebuchadnezzar had set up. . . . 4And the herald proclaimed aloud, "You are commanded, O peoples, nations, and languages, 5that when you hear the sound of . . . music, you are to fall down and worship the golden image that King Nebuchadnezzar has set up; 6and whoever does not fall down and worship shall immediately be cast into a burning fiery furnace." 7Therefore, as soon as all the peoples heard the sound of . . . music, all the peoples, nations, and languages fell down and worshiped the golden image which King Nebuchadnezzar had set up.

8Therefore at that time certain Chaldeans came forward and maliciously accused the Jews. 9They said to King Nebuchadnezzar, "O king, live for ever! . . . 12There are certain Jews whom you have appointed over the affairs of the province of Babylon: Shadrach, Meshach, and Abednego. These men, O king, pay no heed to you; they do not serve your gods or worship the golden image which you have set up."

13Then Nebuchadnezzar in furious rage commanded that Shadrach, Meshach, and Abednego be brought. Then they brought these men before the king. 14Nebuchadnezzar said to them, Is it true, O Shadrach, Meshach, and Abednego, that you do not serve my gods or worship the golden image which I have set up? 15Now if you are ready when you hear the sound of . . . music, to fall down and worship the image which I have made, well and good; but

if you do not worship, you shall immediately be cast into
a burning fiery furnace; and who is the god that will
deliver you out of my hands?"

    [16]Shadrach, Meshach, and Abednego answered the
king, "O Nebuchadnezzar, we have no need to answer you
in this matter. [17]If it be so, our God whom we serve is able
to deliver us from the burning fiery furnace; and he will
deliver us out of your hand, O king. [18]But if not, be it
known to you, O king, that we will not serve your gods
or worship the golden image which you have set up."

There are two problems with this condensation. First and less
significant, the ellipses are a bother. We wonder what has been
left out and whether it is important. All they replace, however,
are long, repetitive lists of musical instruments and functionaries that may adorn the style of the narrative but are inconse-
quential to its substance. Those who want the full flavor of both
style and substance can read the whole chapter aloud. It will
take some breath control and is best done sitting down.

Second, and more significant, the text stops midstream. We
get to the most exciting part, where we are asking breathlessly,
"What happens next? Do they get burned alive or do they
escape?" and the text, as printed here, fails us. There is a reason
for this premature closure, which will emerge in the course of
our study.

Whatever else the book of Daniel has later come to mean, it
was originally a "tract for the times," a way of bolstering Jewish
faith and resistance during the terrible reign of Antiochus Epi-
phanes (ca. 168 B.C.), a ruler who claimed to be "God manifest"
and set up an altar to Zeus in the Temple in Jerusalem. This
story, set in the earlier time of King Nebuchadnezzar, was a
veiled way of addressing the tribulation through which Jewish
readers were going during their own lifetimes. Anyone who
knew the code (for "Nebuchadnezzar" read "Antiochus Epi-
phanes") would also find the story as contemporary as the
Jerusalem *Post* and the evening news bulletins just before *All in*

the Family. The plot is straightforward; the characters are clearly drawn, if a bit stereotypical (a power-hungry monarch, subservient subjects, clean-living Jewish boys); the implications are staggering.

Nebuchadnezzar is feeling insecure. Tribute money has dropped 7.3 percent during the last quarter of the current fiscal year, and there have been some uprisings in one of the outlying provinces. An editorial in the Babylonian *Register* has hinted, ever so gently, that the king is over the hill. No problem about a repeat on the editorial page; the editor was liquidated within an hour after the early morning edition hit the streets. But still . . .

So the king designs a ceremony to "draw the country back together"—around himself. A huge gold statue is installed in a public park where it can be seen for miles around. Everybody is commanded not only to appear for the dedication ceremony but also to fall down and worship the image. Is the image that of Nebuchadnezzar or a god? The distinction is academic. By bowing down to the image, whoever it represents, the people are really bowing down to Nebuchadnezzar and saying by their action, "O King, live forever; we will do whatever you command us."

Of course, they have a vested interest in doing what the king-who-will-live-forever commands them, for certain conditions have been laid out in advance with admirable clarity. The king, wanting to be fair to his subjects, gives them a choice: they can choose to worship the idol (in which case all will be well) or they can choose *not* to worship the idol (in which case all will not be well and they will be cast into a burning fiery furnace). It is a source of gratification to the king that virtually all his subjects, in an exercise of free will between the options just cited, choose to honor his request. With such widespread sentiments of steadfast loyalty he can begin to breathe easily again.

"Virtually all his subjects" obey, but not quite all. For, unknown to the king, there are three who refuse to comply with the order—three of those perennial engagers in noncompliance, the Jews.

How does the king find this out? The way any government finds out about dissidents and threats to law and order: Enter the informers.

Some Chaldeans, professional soothsayers, with a chip on their collective shoulders, slyly inform the king that there is trouble afoot close to the center of power. Three of his most trusted civil servants, Shadrach, Meshach, and Abednego, who only last month had their security clearance renewed, have not only refused to serve Nebuchadnezzar's gods but also will not worship the golden image he has set up.

The men are summoned into the presence of the furious monarch, who decides that this is no time for negotiation. He must hang tough and show who's boss. He gives it to them straight: either they fall down and worship the golden image pronto or it's the burning fiery furnace for all three. And then, convinced that he has the upper hand, Nebuchadnezzar toys with them; he will indulge a theological discussion. Query: "Who is the god that will deliver you out of my hands?"

Shadrach, Meshach, and Abednego, who must have realized early that noncompliance was a rocky road, are prepared for a theological exchange even with the one who holds their lives in the balance. They make three crisp points, each more important than its predecessor:

1. We really don't feel compelled to answer your question.
2. Nevertheless we inform you, O king, that the God we serve is able to deliver us not only from the fiery furnace but out of your hands as well.

They have given about as straight an answer as can be imagined, but, before the king can offer a personally guided tour to the door of the fiery furnace, they add:

3. "But if not . . . " (even if our God does not deliver us from the fiery furnace or from your hands), "we will not serve your gods or worship the golden image which you have set up."

This is a lot straighter answer than Nebuchadnezzar, or anyone else in the court (especially the Chaldean informers), could have imagined. They will remain true to their God, no matter what the circumstances, and the circumstances are likely to change dramatically within seconds. But in the changing circumstances they opt for unchanging allegiance.

End of episode.

But it really isn't fair to leave the story dangling. The pace quickens and the plot heats up, literally. The king orders the furnace heated to seven times its normal temperature. Leaving nothing to chance, he orders Shadrach, Meshach, and Abednego to be bound, fully dressed, and tossed into the furnace. In an ironic touch, the heat is now so intense that the men who throw them into the furnace are themselves consumed by the flames.

And from there on it's a plot almost straight enough for the *Reader's Digest.* Not a hair on the heads of Shadrach, Meshach, and Abednego is even singed. They have a heavenly visitant, a fourth person, "like a son of the gods," whom the king observes walking with them in the midst of the flames. (Apparently Nebuchadnezzar had a heat-resistant peephole through which he could savor the delectable experience of watching his enemies roast.) Since in this case no roasting ensues, the amazed king orders the men to come out of the furnace. It is the first royal command they seem inclined to obey.

The king is persuaded by the exhibition; their God really has saved them. And so, still hedging his theological bets, Nebuchadnezzar, while not affirming their God, issues a decree that anyone who says anything against the God of Shadrach, Meshach, and Abednego shall be—not thrown into a fiery furnace, since that's no longer a fail-safe deterrent, but torn limb from limb. The loose ends are quickly tied together. Shadrach, Meshach, and Abednego get their government security clearance reinstated, their jobs back, and a raise in pay, and Blue Cross, and taking their special circumstances into account, gives them unlimited medical coverage.

The Hollywood ending strains our credulity, for we know that life has a habit of failing to measure up to such scenarios. But the Hollywood ending is cited for a specific reason: When Shadrach, Meshach, and Abednego make their forthright declaration ("Our God whom we serve is able to deliver us from the burning fiery furnace; and he will deliver us out of your hand, O king. *But if not,* be it known to you, O king, that we will not serve your gods or worship the golden image which you have set up"), *they have no assurance of a Hollywood ending.* God gives no guarantees in advance. Their very phrase "But if not . . ." is their way of saying, "We don't know whether we will survive or not. We are not affirming belief in God as a bargaining chip to save us from the fiery furnace. Whether we survive or not is not the issue. The issue is that we remain faithful to God."

Having been entertained by the ending, we can lay it aside. The point of the story is found in the words, "But if not . . ."

OTHER BIBLICAL PASSAGES

Most of us would prefer to avoid such either/or alternatives. We could surely have worked out an agreement between king and commoners without having to jeopardize three such promising lives. Unfortunately, the Bible takes a dim view of such maneuvers:

1. During the persecution of the early church under Domitian, another "code book," the book of Revelation, was circulated. Its early chapters contain a series of letters to churches; and the final letter to the church of Laodicea, with words attributed to Jesus, is stern:

> I know your works: you are neither cold nor hot. Would
> that you were cold or hot! So, because you are lukewarm,
> and neither cold nor hot, I will spew you out of my mouth.
> (Rev. 3:15–16)

What did the Laodiceans have going for them to make it possible to heed such harsh words? Only a future hope, that the One
who spoke the harsh words also meant it when he said, a few
lines later:

> Behold, I stand at the door and knock; if any hear my
> voice and open the door, I will come in and eat with them,
> and they with me. (Rev. 3:20, adapted)

2. The passages in Daniel and Revelation presuppose a God
who is eminently trustable, although there are no guarantees in
advance that such trust pays off. The experience of Abraham
and Sarah further illustrates this difficult truth. Abraham and
Sarah had it made—many flocks, many wells, many servants, a
lovely place to live. And then God, who also (as Woody Allen
reminds us) sometimes speaks in a clear, well-modulated voice,
gave Abraham a clear, well-modulated message: put all your
security up for grabs, shake the dust off your feet, hit the road,
and I'll lead you to an even better place. The letter to the
Hebrews, in more nuanced cadences, continues the tale:

> By faith Abraham and Sarah obeyed when they were
> called to go out to a place which they were to receive as
> an inheritance; and they went out, *not knowing where they*
> *were to go.* By faith they *sojourned* in the land of *promise*,
> as in a *foreign land*, living in *tents*. (Heb. 11:8–9, adapted)

The italicized words all signal the uncertainty of the venture.
We know from where we stand that it was a wise move. *But they*
didn't. To Abraham and Sarah it was the gamble of a lifetime.
Their only assurance in undertaking such a wild goose chase is
suggested in the next verse, and even it represents future hope
rather than present fact: They "looked forward to the city which

has foundations, whose builder and maker is God" (Heb. 11:10).

3. Not even Jesus was exempt from uncertainty. In the garden of Gethsemane, just moments before his arrest, all Jesus knew was that the enemy was closing in and that torture and death were coming next. And so, not unnaturally, he asked God to cancel the script and substitute a new one: "If it be possible, let this cup [of suffering] pass from me . . ." (Matt. 26:39b).

That prayer was no charade. When someone is "sweating blood" (Luke 22:44) as Jesus is, it's not a game. Like Shadrach, Meshach, and Abednego—like Abraham and Sarah—Jesus has no assurance that all will be well. But, also like them, he has the assurance of Someone in whom he trusts—One whom he trusts enough so that, after a pause, he can continue, ". . . nevertheless, not as I will, but as thou wilt" (Matt. 26:39c).

ITEMS FOR REFLECTION AND DISCUSSION

We are at the heart of what is most fundamental about biblical faith in God. It is *trust,* trust despite contrary evidence, trust in scorn of consequences. Fortunately, such "unchanging allegiance" to God is not limited to biblical characters:

1. Now in those days King Adolf made a graven image called a swastika. And he summoned all the members of his party, all the leaders of his government, all the officers and enlisted personnel of his military forces, all the teachers, all the businessmen, all the church members, and he said to them, "This image, and my person, represent a new era for our country. When you greet one another you shall say 'Heil Hitler!' And when you leave one another you shall say 'Heil Hitler!' In every home, in every church, in every place of business, in every classroom, you shall display the swastika and my picture, and for them you shall be prepared to make any sacrifice, even of life itself. And whoever does not do so shall be sent to a burning fiery furnace or a gas chamber."

And the people did as he commanded them, and worshiped

the images he had set up, and behold, the few who did not do so were sent to the burning fiery furnaces and the gas chambers.

But it came to pass that informers came to him and said, "Heil Hitler! There are certain people, beloved leader, who do not worship as you command."

And he said to them, "Who are they?" And they said, "The Jews, beloved leader. And what is more, they claim to worship a different God from yours."

Then Hitler was in a furious rage and said, "We know already of these people, and how they contaminate life and debase the blood of our race. Since, therefore, they worship another God and will not bow down to our god, and since they have always been a pestilence on the earth, let us send them *all* to the fiery furnaces and the gas chambers and rid the earth of them forever." And he commanded new fiery furnaces and gas chambers to be built especially to destroy the Jews. "And then we will see," he shouted, "whether their God will save them from the burning fiery furnaces and the gas chambers."

And it was as he commanded, and the Jews were shoved into the fiery furnaces and the gas chambers, fifty at a time, then a thousand a day, then ten thousand a day, until a million Jews had been destroyed, and then two million, and finally six million.

And as the Jews went to the burning fiery furnaces and the gas chambers, some went in faith, and some went in disbelief to the very end that such things would happen, and many went with the *Shema Yisroel* on their lips—"Hear, O Israel: The Lord our God, the Lord is one"—their ancient affirmation of faith in the living God. It was their way of saying, "The Lord our God, *Adonai Elohenu,* can save us from the burning fiery furnaces and the gas chambers, *but if not,* be it known to you, O Hitler, that we will not serve your gods or worship the image which you have set up."

But this time no one was saved.

And six million times no one was saved.

And forty years later the *Shema Yisroel* is still on the lips of Jews. . . .

It is a cause for wonder and tears and questions and yearning and angry hope.

2. There is a man in El Salvador who becomes a priest and finally (since he seems moderate and conciliatory) an archbishop. He wants to keep peace in a land where the junta (the military dictators) are torturing and killing not only the peasants but also the priests who help the peasants organize for economic and political change. The junta kills as many as ten thousand ordinary citizens in a single ordinary year.

So the archbishop, whose name is Oscar Ernulfo Romero, begins to speak out against the junta. He writes to the President of the United States (who supports the junta), urging that the United States ship no more guns to the junta murderers. (The guns are still being shipped to this day.) He calls upon the soldiers in the Salvadoran army to disobey orders when told to murder their own kinfolk.

In these and other ways he demonstrates that he is no longer willing to bow down before the junta and worship its gods—its god of "law and order at any price," which means murder; its god of despotic power, which means torture; its god of wealth for the few, which means starvation for the many.

But instead of escorting Archbishop Romero to a burning fiery furnace, the Nebuchadnezzars in El Salvador wait until he is celebrating Mass—worshiping his God rather than the gods of the junta—and they shoot him, leaving his bullet-ridden body prostrate before the altar.

His story remains a story in the present tense because, as he predicted, Oscar Ernulfo Romero has risen in the hearts of the Salvadoran people.

3. In another part of Latin America, a sixteen-year-old non-Christian with the very Christian name of Maria becomes involved in a "base community," one of thousands of such groups all over the continent who meet for prayer, Bible study, and

social action, with a heavy enough emphasis on the "social action" so that their lives are always in danger. After a time, Maria wants to be baptized and confirmed. But the priest demurs. He thinks it might be better to wait a little longer for Maria to join the church, until she has matured more fully. "I'm not sure," says the priest, "that Maria is yet ready to die for her faith."

By her eighteenth birthday, Maria has been baptized and confirmed and has died for her faith.

Such tales are soul-stirring, but they seem existentially, as well as geographically, far removed from us. *We* don't live in such desperate circumstances. Nobody is telling *us* to bow down and worship idols.

Or is that quite the case? Here are three random examples closer to home:

• Our army invades another country, thereby breaking treaties and ignoring previously signed international agreements, and when the United Nations votes 109–8 to "deplore" our illegal action, the man who is President and Commander in Chief of the Armed Forces remarks that this vote of almost unanimous censure by the rest of the world "didn't disturb my breakfast one bit."

• Legislation is enacted that, according to one report, will require "all government officials with access to high-level classified information, *for the rest of their lives,* to submit for governmental review, newspaper articles or books they write for the general reading public." The purpose, as a commentator puts it, "is to prevent unauthorized disclosure of classified information, but its effects are likely to go far beyond that. It will give those in power a new and powerful weapon to delay or even suppress criticism by those most knowledgeable to voice it" (Floyd Abrams, "The New Effort to Control Information," *The New York Times Magazine,* Sept. 25, 1983, p. 22, italics added).

• An eighteen-year-old boy, who feels that in conscience he cannot register for the military draft, is liable to receive a sentence of five years in jail.

Respond to the following assessment: Although these are not examples of sending people to fiery furnaces or gas chambers, they are initial steps down a road that could finally lead there. They are ways of saying, "Don't disagree with those of us in power. If you do, we'll either (as the above examples show) ignore you, or force you to keep quiet, or send you to jail. And don't press your luck, because in the interests of 'national security' we are prepared to move to sterner measures if necessary."

In wartime we hear, "There are no atheists in foxholes." A more accurate statement would be, whether in wartime or peacetime, "There are no atheists—" period. The Daniel story is not about people who believe in God versus people who don't. It's a story about people who *believe in different gods.*

Most of us are probably polytheists, people who believe in several gods—the god to whom we give our verbal allegiance, and then the other values, projects, loyalties, persons, on whom we are willing to lavish a lot of uncritical loyalty and for whom we might be willing to deny everything else.

A list of gods *we* might acknowledge as serious claimants for our allegiance could go like this:

Making the team

Becoming No. 1 (in school, business, politics, world affairs, or stolen bases—anything but strikeouts)

Getting the girl . . . or boy

Taking charge (of the corporation, the political party, the school board, the labor union, the government of a small country)

Stopping the Russians

If we asked our friends in the third world to tell us what gods they perceive us worshiping, really worshiping, no matter what we say our ultimate loyalties are, the list might look something like this:

> Keeping the United States No. 1 at all costs
>
> Maintaining absolute superiority over any other nation in guns, tanks, nuclear weapons
>
> The right to decide who should govern countries that might otherwise "threaten" us
>
> The right to have a "good life" even at the expense of other people or nations
>
> Operating within an economic system that nobody tries to regulate

We may not find such a list flattering to our egos, individual or national, but in our more candid moments we can sometimes admit that such are, indeed, operative "gods" for many within our culture.

And at that point, for those who feel some uneasiness in worshiping such deities, the question is posed: When the power of such gods is so great in our land, how can we risk affirming the God of Shadrach, Meshach, and Abednego, of Abraham, Sarah, Jesus, the Jews, Archbishop Romero, Maria? Such an act of faith seems a very long shot: no assurances, no guarantees— and even the odds aren't particularly appealing (sometimes six million to none). Such a God can save us from the power of the other gods, but then again, such a God might not. . . .

A struggle with that dilemma will characterize the rest of our lives, if we are serious about it. All we can do in conclusion here is to make a modest beginning:

We can begin by remembering that if faith in this God is risky, none of the other gods offer built-in guarantees either. The choice is never between a risk and a sure thing. *It's always a choice between risks.* There is never a sure thing any more than there is ever a free lunch.

We can also remember that if belief in such a God entails risk, there's some consistency on the scene, because the God we are talking about is a risk-taking God. The God of Abraham, Isaac, and Jacob, and of Sarah, Leah, and Rachel, is always in the thick of things, siding with the poor, putting the divine name on the line for a bunch of slaves, and—in Christian terms—getting incarnated in the most unlikely and risky way imaginable, in a first-century Jew who lived at a time (like all times) when people in general didn't like Jews very much and people in power didn't like Jews at all. So if we get in trouble for affirming such a God, we can be sure that Trouble is God's middle name and that such a God will be alongside us in the midst of trouble, rather than off in a remote heaven practicing neutrality.

And if we can begin to make that most difficult switch of all —away from the gods of middle-class values and upward mobility and gilt-edged retirement plans—and if we can explore, even tentatively and gingerly, what it would be like to think with and act for those who are the victims, we might just uncover the most "unexpected news" of all: that God got there before we did.

AN EPILOGUE:
FOR THOSE WHO FEEL
PERSONALLY ASSAULTED

We have examined passages typical of biblical emphases that we tend to ignore. Obviously there are other biblical emphases. But they are *in addition to*, rather than antithetical to, those we have examined. We may supplement what is here with other biblical materials, but we cannot obliterate the themes here developed without distorting the biblical message.

Where does this leave middle-class, well-intentioned, sincerely committed mainline church folk? If we are still listening, it leaves us battered, wounded, macerated. It may also leave us resentful and angry at being assaulted from a different direction in every chapter. "This is good news?" we feel like responding. "If so, who needs it? Just because we are not starving, we are supposed to feel guilty? Does our country never do anything right? Is being poor and third world all that counts? Is the Bible nothing but a put-down of who we are?"

Since I, too, am not immune from such feelings, let me share some responses.

1. It is appropriate that anyone's first reaction to the "good news" should be to find it bad news, because the condition of receiving the good news is *change* (what the Bible calls *metanoia*, "conversion"). To be told that we need to change is to be told that we are presently unsatisfactory. So the admonition to change is always bad news, making us uncomfortable and defensive.

The apostle Peter provides us with some company. When he first met Jesus his response was not "Well, glad you have finally appeared on the scene to give us the good news." It was "Leave me alone. You're asking more than I care to give" (or, in an earlier translation, "Depart from me, for I am a sinful man, O Lord").

So if our initial confrontation with the biblical message leaves us uncomfortable, we are not alone; it goes with the territory of being a Christian. The thing to feel uncomfortable about would be if we didn't feel uncomfortable.

2. We should also realize that the source of our discomfort is not third world Christians trying to put us down. It is not *they* who are giving us a bad time; rather, *the Bible* is giving us a bad time. They have not created a new biblical message to make us feel guilty; they are only calling attention to the old biblical message we have camouflaged for centuries in order not to feel guilty. In ancient times a king would sometimes kill the messenger who brought bad news—which showed that the king had failed to locate the source of his problem and also led to a high absentee rate among messengers in time of crisis. No need to perpetuate the king's mistake today.

(I make this point with a degree of self-interest, since some readers may perceive me as saying through these pages, "*I* say that *you* are uncaring." I can only reply that I feel as much indicted by the biblical message as any reader, and perhaps more so, since the themes of this book have plagued me for several years and I have not set a particularly stunning track record for change in the interval. While I am not rich, I am certainly not poor; my income, even though I cannot live within it, is princely compared to that of most of the rest of the world; my home, if not large, is ample; my larder, if not lavishly stocked, is far from bare. So when readers feel personally indicted, let them know that the author stands among them.)

3. About the presumed "attacks" on the United States we can be brief. We are not immediately responsible for the policies of

the Russians or the Chinese; we *are* immediately responsible for the policies of the United States. Our initial and strongest critique must be directed at ourselves. If we are honest at that point, we earn the right to focus our critique elsewhere, and must do so. But there is a priority. Critiques of "Russia" are often ways of blowing a smokescreen over our own shortcomings.

Much of the critique, moreover, is justified. This is not only the way we are perceived by many third world Christians (which in itself would be sufficient reason for us to listen carefully), it also describes the way we do in fact behave a great deal of the time. To refer to certain dictators as "U.S.-backed" is, unhappily, merely a statement of fact. If we morally abhor the fact, we must change the circumstance that produces it. When we think the critique unjustified, we must be able to appeal for vindication to the *actions* of our government and not just to statements of good intentions.

The nation is the most pervasive of all the gods, in any time, in any culture. True patriotism is not worship of our nation but rather, in the light of our worship of the God of justice, to conform our nation's ways to justice. Albert Camus once wrote, "I should like to love my country and still love justice." That will always be a worthy, and a necessary, aspiration.

4. When "personal assault" is the topic, we need to recall some things said earlier about systemic evil. It is true that some folk (the minority who are like us) benefit lavishly from the socio-political-economic system under which we live, while others (the majority who are not like us) are crushed and destroyed by it. But this is not the same as saying that corporation officials sit in their boardrooms saying, "Let's figure out a way to make greater profits so that children will starve." What they *are* saying, if they are playing by their corporations' rules, is, "Let's figure out a way to make greater profits." And the tragedy is that the way they make greater profits may have the unintended consequences that children do starve or dictators are supported,

since dictators can "maintain social stability"—a euphemism for exercising whatever power is necessary to keep workers from organizing for better wages, since better wages will mean lower profits. The problem is not so much that a few powerful people with evil intentions get their way as that a few powerful people *with good intentions* may, quite contrary to those intentions, produce evil ends.

This means that the "victims" are not only those who get physically ground to pieces or starve but also sensitive people whom the system forces to act in ways that destroy others, even though they wish it didn't. It is important for such people to begin to realize that *they* are being manipulated and thus dehumanized: they are put in situations where they cannot make the business decisions they would like to make but are forced, if they wish to survive in business, to implement corporate policies of which they do not personally approve.

If any of them are readers of this book, I hope they can hear this not as a new assault on their persons but as a tiny hint of the possibility of liberation for themselves from the need to spend the rest of their lives beholden to false gods. They could then approach the biblical materials afresh, realizing that beyond the stings of indictment lie the birthpangs of hope.

5. The great hope, surely, is that we *can* begin to be liberated from some of the false gods—the Bible calls them "idols"—that have held us in captivity. We know their names: fear of change, the need to conform, the burden of success expectations programmed into us from childhood, the stigma of being thought "unpatriotic," the terror of becoming vulnerable. All these gods urge us to refrain from asking such questions as "Isn't there something wrong when our allegiances physically destroy our sisters and brothers elsewhere and at the same time psychically destroy us too?"

If we could face the question of the effects our allegiances have, we could begin the painful but necessary process the Bible talks about, that of "changing sides." We could begin to reread and reappropriate the long heritage that is ours, preserved in the book we have been studying, enshrined also in our history and our tradition, but always more powerful than any of the vessels in which it is contained, more powerful even than our own attempts to reduce it to nonthreatening platitudes.

When we face that question, we are ready as never before to hear—as if for the first time—the earliest words recorded in Jesus' ministry: "The time is fulfilled, and the kingdom of God is at hand; repent and believe the good news" (Mark 1:15).

BIBLIOGRAPHY:
WHERE TO READ FROM HERE

The British writer Charles Williams once remarked that in seeking to understand the book of Job there were many commentaries and exegetical works available, and in their absence even the book itself could be consulted.

The important bibliographical resource to which this book points is, of course, the Bible itself. To penetrate beyond its familiar cadences and discover "unexpected news," a variety of translations will help. If group study is being done, try to have at least the following available: *The Good News Bible, The Jerusalem Bible, The Revised Standard Version, The New English Bible.* Individual translations of portions of the Bible, such as J. B. Phillips' translation of the New Testament (1958; rev. ed. 1972) and Clarence Jordan's *Cotton Patch Version* (4 vols., including most of the New Testament; Association Press, 1963–73) will also help. It is an obvious advantage if any members of the group know Hebrew or Greek, but make sure they allow group discussion to move beyond purely philological questions.

LATIN AMERICAN RESOURCES

The greatest help in confronting "unexpected" dimensions of the passages will come from studying writings by third world Christians who approach the texts with different presuppositions than our own. The following are a few Latin American resources that can help in this endeavor. Those starred (*) are the ones to which I have referred most frequently.

Boff, Leonardo. *The Lord's Prayer: The Prayer of Integral Liberation.* Orbis Books, 1983.

An example of starting with our own situation and showing, phrase by phrase, how the Lord's Prayer speaks of "the *integral* liberation of human beings, not just of their spiritual liberation."

Cardenal, Ernesto. *The Psalms of Struggle and Liberation.* Herder & Herder, 1971.
Cardenal's own paraphrases of twenty-five biblical psalms speak directly to "struggle and liberation" in Central America.

*———. *The Gospel in Solentiname.* 4 vols. Orbis Books, 1976–82.
Each Sunday in the village of Solentiname, Nicaragua (later totally destroyed by the U.S.-backed Somoza forces), Fr. Cardenal led a discussion of the Gospel lesson rather than giving a sermon. The four volumes are transcriptions of these group efforts and illustrate the actual *doing* of Bible study. They contain the quiet eloquence of the uneducated who see profundities hidden from the "wise."

Croatto, J. Severino. *Exodus: A Hermeneutics of Freedom.* Orbis Books, 1981.
A serious treatment of new approaches to biblical study, focusing on the exodus and relating that examination to the creation stories, the Hebrew prophets, Jesus, and Paul.

*Gutiérrez, Gustavo. *A Theology of Liberation.* Orbis Books, 1973.
The most important single book for understanding "liberation theology," containing over four hundred biblical references.

———. *The Power of the Poor in History.* Orbis Books, 1983.
Recent essays that show the continuing centrality of the Bible. (*Note:* An entire book of biblical studies by Gutiérrez, *El Dios de la Vida,* will soon be in English.)

*Miranda, José Porfirio. *Marx and the Bible.* Orbis Books, 1974.
North American readers should not be put off by the title. The bulk of the volume is detailed exegesis of central biblical texts. See chapter 2 in particular, "The God of the Bible."

———. *Being and the Messiah.* Orbis Books, 1977.
Deals with the message of the Fourth Gospel from a "liberation" perspective. Exegetical material begins in chapter 4.

———. *Communism in the Bible.* Orbis Books, 1982.
A compact (85-page) blockbuster that looks at the "communistic" structure of the early church in Acts (2:44–45) and reexamines Jesus' teachings in the light of it.

Segundo, Juan Luis. *The Liberation of Theology.* Orbis Books, 1976.
While mainly a treatment of theological method, the book (especially chapter 1 on "The Hermeneutical Circle") suggests new ways to use Scripture without cheating.

*Tamez, Elsa. *Bible of the Oppressed.* Orbis Books, 1982.
Exemplifies the careful exegetical work being done in Latin America in relating biblical motifs (in this case "oppression" and "liberation") to a socioeconomic view of the world in which the oppressed live.

RESOURCES FROM THE NORTHERN HEMISPHERE

Biblical scholarship in the northern hemisphere has not widely used liberation themes as a way to examine the biblical world and the modern world. There are, however, a few exceptions:

Brueggemann, Walter. *The Prophetic Imagination.* Fortress Press, 1978.
Particularly suggestive in showing how "the alternative community of Moses" challenged "the royal consciousness" (of Pharaoh), this book provides resources for prophetic criticizing and prophetic energizing.

Cassidy, Richard J. *Jesus, Politics, and Society: A Study of Luke's Gospel.* Orbis Books, 1978.
A careful excursion through Luke, giving special attention to Jesus' social stance, and his relation to the political and socioeconomic factors of his time.

Cassidy, Richard J., and Scharper, Philip J., eds. *Political Issues in Luke-Acts.* Orbis Books, 1983.
A variety of scholars pursue issues raised in Cassidy's earlier volume.

Fiorenza, Elisabeth Schüssler. *In Memory of Her.* Crossroad Publishing Co., 1983.
A reconstruction of life and teaching in the early church from a feminist perspective, illustrating how new approaches to the biblical materials can liberate women long oppressed by male scholarship.

Gottwald, Norman K. *The Tribes of Jahweh: A Sociology of the Religion of Liberated Israel, 1250–1050 B.C.* Orbis Books, 1979.
A huge breakthrough, examining portions of the Hebrew Scriptures in the light of socioeconomic analysis.

————, ed. *The Bible and Liberation: Politics and Social Hermeneutics.*
Orbis Books, 1983.
A symposium offering sociological readings of the Bible, using class
analysis, political theology, and Marxism.

Pixley, George V. *God's Kingdom.* Orbis Books, 1981.
A brief and readable study of the kingdom of God in Scripture, by
a "gringo" who has identified deeply with the oppressed in Central
America.

Yoder, John Howard. *The Politics of Jesus.* Wm. B. Eerdmans Publishing Co., 1972.
A treatment of Jesus' ministry from a Mennonite perspective that
challenges most conventional interpretations of Jesus. Especially
helpful on the centrality of the Jubilee year.

A bit immodestly, I conclude with two books of my own that explore
in more detail our indebtedness to Latin American Christians:
Theology in a New Key. Westminster Press, 1978.
Gustavo Gutiérrez. John Knox Press, 1980.